Comic Power in Emily Dickinson

Comic Power in *Emily Dickinson*

SUZANNE JUHASZ

CRISTANNE MILLER

MARTHA NELL SMITH

UNIVERSITY OF TEXAS PRESS   AUSTIN

Requests for permission to reproduce material from this work should be sent to Permissions, University of Texas Press, Box 7819, Austin TX 78713-7819.

∞ The paper used in this publication meets the minimum requirements of American National Standard for Information Sciences—Permanence of Paper for Printed Library Materials, ANSI Z39.48-1984.

Library of Congress Cataloging-in-Publication Data

Juhasz, Suzanne, date
    Comic power in Emily Dickinson / Suzanne Juhasz, Cristanne Miller,
Martha Nell Smith. — 1st ed.
        p.   cm.
    Includes bibliographical references (p.) and index.
    ISBN 0-292-74029-8 (alk. paper)
        1. Dickinson, Emily, 1830–1886—Humor.   2. Humorous poetry,
American—History and criticism.   3. Comic, The, in literature.   I. Miller,
Cristanne.   II. Smith, Martha Nell, date.   III. Title.
PS1541.Z5J78   1993
811'.4—dc20   93-786

To Bill, Jerry, and Marilee

Contents

Acknowledgments

WHILE TOO MANY PEOPLE to mention have been supportive of us individually in our writing of this book, we want to give special notice to those individuals and institutions that have provided crucially enabling assistance. We are grateful to Pomona College, the University of Colorado, Boulder, and the University of Maryland, College Park, for their direct and indirect financial support for this project. More specifically, we would like to thank Marie Williamson, Administrative Assistant of the English Department at Pomona College, for her indefatigable work in organizing all the small but essential aspects of manuscript production, and most especially for her computer expertise. Pomona College work-study students Lenora Reynolds, Lisa Lee, and Hilary Younkin have also provided valuable assistance. We are also indebted to Ann Steinecke for her astute proofreading and thorough indexing. Martha Nell Smith would like to thank the National Endowment for the Humanities and the General Research Board of the University of Maryland, for fellowship support, and John Lancaster, Special Collections Curator, Amherst College, and Rodney G. Dennis, former Curator of Manuscripts, Houghton Library of Harvard University, as well as staff members of both libraries for all their help over the years. Special thanks to T. O. Sylvester, for the witty presentation of the comic Emily Dickinson. Finally, our thanks to Barbara Mossberg for her contribution to the generative MLA seminar on Dickinson and Comedy in 1988.

Chapter 1
Comedy and Audience in Emily Dickinson's Poetry

ALTHOUGH EMILY DICKINSON WAS A NOTED WIT in her circle of friends and family, and although her poetry is surely clever, frequently downright funny, and, as we shall argue, throughout possessed of a significant comic vision, criticism has paid little attention to her humor. Dickinson's profound scrutiny of life-and-death matters has usually taken precedence in the analysis and evaluation of her work. Yet comedy is a part of that profundity, and this volume brings the comic aspects of her vision to center stage for the first time. It is no coincidence that feminist critics have chosen this subject, for comedy is aligned with subversive and disruptive modes that offer alternative perspectives on culture. But even as it is a cliché in American social politics that "feminists have no sense of humor," so the comedy specifically associated with women's critique of patriarchy is often overlooked.

A feminist critical approach to Dickinson's comedy reveals a poet whose topic and audience are larger than herself. It shows how Dickinson critiques the established culture through language forms that stress their status as performance and demand the participation of an audience. In particular, focusing on comedy highlights her responses as a nineteenth-century upper-middle-class woman to situations in which she is both attracted to and angered by patriarchal power, situations in which she critiques contemporary institutions, and situations in which she feels suffocated by social conventions. Through formal elements of voice, image, and narrative, Dickinson teases, mocks, even outrages her audience in ways that are akin both to the gestures of traditional comedy and to specifically feminist humor. In short, Dickinson's comedy is not contained by poems that are obviously funny but pervades her writing to offer a transforming vision of the world.

Dickinson the tragedienne, however, has by now received so much press that this role has become a norm in critical representations of her, in feminist as well as traditional readings. George Whicher, setting the tone for contemporary receptions of Dickinson, writes in 1938, "by mastery of her suffering she won a sanity that could make even grief a plaything" (109). Thus, this critical story goes, Dickinson is a heroine *because* she suffered so, and because she gave us great poetry out of this suffering. Not all subsequent critics have been so charitable about the triumph of her fragile sanity, but most agree that her despair and desolation are the crucible in which her poetry is forged. Whicher proposes a compensatory, even therapeutic theory for Dickinson's poetry:

> In projecting her intensest feelings on paper she was finding a form of relief in action; she was, in Emerson's phrase, "grinding into paint" her burden of despair. So she was enabled to fulfill the prescript of her generation for utter rectitude of conduct, which for her meant the stifling of hopes, and yet keep the bitter waters from stagnating in her breast. Though her mental balance was unsteady for some years to come, she achieved and held it.   (109)

Such an approach makes the relation of art to biography a closed circuit. There is no audience; or, more properly, the poet's audience is herself. Life experiences govern the experience that is the poem, mediated only in that the poem is seen not simply to describe but to offer a degree of control over them. Without reference, then, to the performance aspect of the literary act, that is, to the complex function of any poem, such critics end by simplifying not only the affective purpose of the poem but its content as well.

As we might expect, critics who focus on the direct link between biography and poetry are especially prone to emphasize the tragic elements of Dickinson's art. To take three important examples in more recent criticism, John Cody, Paula Bennett, and Vivian Pollak—for all of their ideological differences and notwithstanding the forty-years' span their works cover—have reinforced a sense of Dickinson as tragic heroine. Cody and Bennett, for example, although worlds apart in their conclusions, both follow the lead of Whicher, who notes that "the prolonged nervous tension brought on by falling in love with a man whom she could not marry was almost too much for her" (137), in seeing frustrated romantic experience at the root of psychological trauma and mental collapse. In short, Cody, taking a traditional Freudian approach, finds Dickinson's latent homosexuality a symptom of her psychological disorders; Bennett reads her thwarted homosexuality as an indication that society has frustrated her sense of fulfilled womanhood. Pollak theorizes beyond the specific to the general, finding Dickinson's anxiety to be less a response to specific people in her life than to the gender-determined cultural situation, but she, too, defines a poetry that is "an anxious rationalization of a uniquely neurotic plight" (30).

John Cody, a practicing psychoanalyst, has bequeathed to the history of Dickinson criticism his portrait of Dickinson the Neurotic. The greatness of her art does not alter his clinical diagnosis: her poems "portray faithfully the terror of a mind collapsing under pressures that exceed its endurance" (24). Not only does he repudiate Whicher's idea that the poetry can have any effect on the life, salutary or otherwise, but he maintains that the life was understood by both Dickinson herself and her community as "abnormal" and "tortured." Dickinson's descriptions of "her anxiety-ridden personality and her seclusive way of life" reveal, he says, "the clear implication that she considers herself the victim of irrational and inflexible aberration" (12). To her contemporaries and neighbors she appeared "pathetically withdrawn, eccentric, or insane" (22). For Cody, Dickinson's poetry offers a one-to-one correspondence with her life. "The profoundly disordered undercurrent one senses in the life moves also through the poetry. Desolation, hopelessness, and a fierce and frustrated longing arise from nearly every page" (23). Poetry, then, functions as self-expression, and a self defined by its "psychic devastation" will produce poetry that is similarly demarcated.

Beginning in a place similar to Cody's poet, who is suicidally depressed, "hollow at the core," Paula Bennett's Dickinson manages, through the creation of a fantasy-life that finds expression in the poems, to achieve a self-maturation previously denied to her. Her vocation as woman-poet is what gives her the opportunity, the license to become a "self-defined, self-authorized, and authenticated woman" (82)—that is, "within the limits of her art, if not her life, she finally had achieved the freedom to be wholly sane" (84). In her fantasy reconstruction of her life (her redefinition of herself as bride but also Queen of Suffering) "and in the poetry to which it gave rise, she was able to express for the first time everything she had felt as a woman because she finally had a definition of herself as a woman which was sufficiently large to justify and accommodate these feelings" (83).

In Bennett's paradigm, poetry's relation to biography is still unmediated—the poem expresses what the poet feels—but being a poet rather than a traditional nineteenth-century woman enables her to imagine for herself a different scenario: "a new ontological status: woman-without-being-a-wife" (78). Bennett sees Dickinson's writing before 1861 as suffering from her blocked maturation: "the poetry she wrote [between 1858 and 1861] tends to be narrow, flat, and weak, even as her sense of self—abandoned, wounded, helpless and childlike—was similarly restricted during much of this time" (48). After 1861, after "redefining herself as bride-wife-queen of Calvary, within the context of a fantasy marriage, the poet was able to integrate her feelings of loss, rage, and frustration, feelings that had left her internally divided from adolescence on, and make these feelings ego-syntonic. They became a necessary part of her new definition of self as poet" (83).

In the spirit if not the details of her analysis, Bennett follows Whicher, then, in assigning to poetry the therapeutic role. Given her emphasis on the life-and-death struggle of Dickinson's psyche (the right to the empowerment of maturation rather than the void of unresolved childhood), it is no wonder that Bennett sees nothing particularly comic about Dickinson. Related to her thematic emphasis is, as we have said, a theory of poetry conflated with a theory of personality: for, again, this poetry is solipsistic, both a direct expression of self and directed to the internal audience of the self. The very idea of performance would seem to be antithetical to these critics, because it undercuts the notion of poetry as spontaneous response to powerful emotions.

For Vivian Pollak, it is not so much a given lover, be it Susan Dickinson or Charles Wadsworth, who is the occasion for the fact that Dickinson is "the laureate of sexual despair" (19); rather, it is her gendered cultural situation writ large. "Dickinson understood her sexuality as both a social and a biological limitation; her poems reveal a mind intent on testing the consequences of a partial severance from this historical given" (25). From this perspective, however, Pollak also emphasizes suffering, pain, conflict, disease, and, most of all, frustration. "Most of Emily Dickinson's poetry, and all of it that matters, originates in frustration" (9).

Pollak is particularly insistent to counter the notion that Dickinson's was a life lived in language with a different opinion about the function of her poems. "Dickinson's achievement as an autobiographical poet privileges her experience as an exceptional woman, rather than her status as a poet working within an established tradition. Nor is it primarily as a poet that Dickinson wishes to be understood . . . Instead, she wishes to be understood as a woman in quest of a vocation: a woman unable to translate her vocation—'ecstasy'—into a more limited experience of it" (123). Again, she tells us: "Her poems are thus not in quest of a subject (her subject is herself) but in quest of an object. This object is a relationship other than her relationship to language that will maximize her sense of personal freedom" (132). The poems are no solution, then; rather, they are an expression of the problem: "social powerlessness is Dickinson's most thoroughly explored, consistently interesting, and intransigently feminist theme" (132). Linking language firmly to lived experience in this way again obscures the comedic elements in Dickinson's work.

Of all the recent advocates for Dickinson as tragedienne, Sandra Gilbert and Susan Gubar do pay primary attention to poetry as performance: "Indeed, art is not so much *poesis*—making—as it is *mimesis*—enactment, and this because she believes that even consciousness is not so much reflective as it is theatrical" (586). As such their work comes closest to the approach in this book. And yet their "woman white" is in no way a comic turn. For although they maintain that the roles Dickinson plays in her romantic drama or Gothic novel "helped her to free herself from social and psychological constraints which might otherwise have stifled or crippled her art," their analysis focuses upon the psychic fragmentation that her various roles revealed and indeed, helped to affirm.

> That Dickinson's white dress implies not a single supposed person but a series of characters suggests, however, not just the artful complexity of her strategy for escaping Requirements but also the dangers implicit in that strategy. Impersonating simultaneously a "little maid" in white, a fierce virgin in white, a nun in white, a bride in white, a mad woman in white, a dead woman in white, and a ghost in white, Dickinson seems to have split herself into a series of incubae, haunting not just her father's house but her own mind.   (621–622)

In other words, this is théâtre vérité, projecting and reifying the mind's interior drama, indicating "Dickinson's keen awareness that she was living (or more accurately, constructing) her life as if it were a gothic romance, and it comments upon the real significance of the gothic genre, especially for women: its usefulness in providing metaphors for those turbulent psychological states into which the divided selves of the nineteenth century so often fell" (624–625). Dickinson's dramatics are tragedy rather than comedy, because they offer reification but not revision of her life: "What was habit in the sense of costume became habit in the more pernicious sense of addiction, and finally the two habits led to both an inner and outer in*habit*ation—a haunting interior *and* an inescapable prison" (591).

We do not argue here that there are no tragic elements in Dickinson's life or art. We take issue, however, with the totality or one-dimensionality of the position. It edits out the wry, the witty, the playful, the tough, the challenging, the successful Dickinson. Moreover, it takes Dickinson all too literally, ignoring her own directives about reading and writing: "Tell all the Truth but tell it slant–/ Success in Circuit lies" (1129). Telling it slant implies the participation in the poetic act of voice, gesture, posture, attitude, and style. It implies, in other words, the necessity of performance, so that the poem cannot be seen as *simply* the compulsive outpouring of powerful feelings. Life experience—all the Truth—has been crafted and shaped for some purpose, and a corollary to the fact that the words are performed is that some audience is anticipated. The poem's affective purpose has to do with a reader as well as with the poet herself.[1]

Comedy becomes possible in a poetics of this kind. To begin with, comedy stresses the role of the audience and its response to the joke. Additionally, comedy implies commentary: the comedienne's art is always slant, never wholly caught up in a feeling or a situation. From this perspective we can see how Dickinson critiques her subject as much as she embodies it. Comedy implies, as well, winning rather than losing, the affirmation of life rather than its destruction. These elements do exist in Dickinson's poetry, and taking her slant, or allowing for her comic perspective, enables us to experience them.

Although we have spoken thus far only of comedy, we are concerned with the whole range of production in Dickinson's work subsumed under that umbrella term: formal comic structures, humor, wit, teasing, parody, visual and verbal cartooning, the grotesque, satire, and so on. Each of us examines different aspects of the verbal or visual play associated with both comedy and humor as strategies that the poet manipulates in order to portray aspects of her world in incongruous and rebellious if not always outright funny forms. The distinctions between these terms, while interesting, do not affect the unity of our conclusions or explorations. Moreover, we have found that writers on women's or feminist work tend not to distinguish as sharply between comedy and humor as writers on traditional comic forms have. Feminist critics typically see both comedy and humor as containing the open-ended, ultimately more radical and explosive social critique previously associated with humor alone.

Umberto Eco, in "The Frames of Comic 'Freedom,'" an essay on traditional comedy and humor, distinguishes comedy as the form that *contains* rule-breaking, diabolic, tabooed, or non-human behavior. In comedy, we enjoy seeing the "animal-like individual" perform at the same time that we rejoice in this figure's punishment (2). The frame of the comedy, the rule to be overthrown, is presupposed rather than explicitly stated but nonetheless essential: comedy depends upon the breaking of some rule or law, and then on the implied reinstatement of that same law. Like "Carnival," comedy, Eco argues, exists as "an *authorized* transgression." Both phenomena "represent paramount examples of law reinforcement. They remind us of the existence of the rule" by requiring the firm assumption of that rule as the norm against which they play (6). Humor, on the contrary, Eco states, calls the frame itself into question:

> In comedy we laugh at the character. In humor we smile because of the contradiction between the character and the frame the character cannot comply with. But we are no longer sure that it is the character who is at fault. Maybe the frame is wrong . . . Humor acts as a form of social criticism . . . through verbal language or some other sign system it casts in doubt other cultural codes. If there is a possibility of transgression, it lies in humor rather than in comic. (8)

This view of the comic stems from readings of ancient comedies and an understanding of their formal structures. From this perspective, comedy takes place at the level of narrative structures; again, in contrast, "humor works in the interstices between narrative and discursive structures." For this reason, humor does not "pretend . . . to lead us beyond our own limits," nor does it promise liberation, the impossible, ultimate escape from law. Instead, it "undermines limits from inside," warns against the optimism of believing in any ultimate escape, and in so doing "makes us feel the uneasiness of living under a law—any law" (8).

Neil Schmitz, who writes only of humor, sees the (primarily masculine) tradition of humor in the United States as being quite similar to what Eco describes. American humorous texts, he argues, tend to "set us adrift . . . [in] a spacious anti-Aristotelian, anti-patriarchal sense of the world, which does not fall discursively into the trap of counter-statement, or mirroring argument" (12). American humorists are skeptical of irony and indeed of "any discourse based on authority," choosing instead a primarily "redemptive" humor (11). The humorist, like the slave of the Hegelian dialectic, knows that no mastery is absolute and celebrates this knowledge. Humor belongs to this slave or underdog, and takes the experience of pain, loss, or suffering as its primary subject (127–131). Despite this insight, however, Schmitz apparently sees humorous production in the United States as almost exclusively male until the twentieth century, where he turns to the work of Gertrude Stein.

Recent feminist studies of women's comedy and humor call primary attention to the subversive, indirect nature of comic production for reasons beyond those of Eco and Schmitz. Because women have been stereotyped as lacking a sense of humor, women who write comedy suffer an intensification of the ordinary prejudices against women who write. Thus, in *A Very Serious Thing: Women's Humor and American Culture*, Nancy Walker—the most prolific writer on women's and feminist humor—

points out that part of the problem in constructing a tradition or acknowledged field of women's humor is contextual: women's wit typically has its
broadest field of play in all-female spheres like the kitchen or the parlor,
but there are cultural sanctions against it in public (that is, predominantly
male) spheres like public speaking and publishing. Because men do not
typically see women's humor, they assume it does not exist. When they do
see it, they do not interpret it as humor—partly because women are
known not to be funny, and partly because the stereotype of the humorist
directly conflicts with that of the woman. While the humorist is aggressive, critical, public in "his" exercise of wit, women have been assumed
to be accepting, generous, modest in their refusal of certain kinds of lime-
light. Although, as Walker demonstrates, women have been publishing
humorous writing for hundreds of years in the United States alone,
stereotypes of women's humorlessness have continued far past Emily
Dickinson's lifetime.

Referring early in her book to Eco's distinctions between humor and
comedy, Walker first eschews making such distinctions herself, focusing
instead more on sociological and cultural than on formal distinctions.
Women's humorous writing, she claims, like that of dominant racial and
ethnic minorities, has had a different relationship to the dominant culture
from that of white men. Because women have to cope with the status quo
as given—not as one of a set of "interchangeable realities" that they could
at any moment choose to enter—their humor tends to be subversive in its
release of the aggression common to all humor (11, 12). "The established
tradition in American humor is replete with tall tales, political satire, and
absurdity; women's humor presents not boasters but victims of cultural expectations . . . and the absurdity they present is the fundamental absurdity
of oppression . . . women writers have developed forms suited to their
own lives and needs" (12).[2] According to Walker's argument, dominant
in American women's humor is the theme of "how it feels to be a member of a subordinate group in a culture that prides itself on equality" (x).

Walker implies in her introduction that humor rather than comedy is
the more inclusive term for the type of writing she describes: for women,
she argues, humor functions "more as a means of communication than as
a means of self-presentation, a sharing of experience rather than a demonstration of cleverness. Related to this is the fact that women's humorous
expression is almost never purely comic or absurd, but instead constitutes
a 'double' or subversive text. Even when, as is frequently the case, it points
to the myriad absurdities that women have been forced to endure in this
culture, it carries with it not the lighthearted feeling that is the privilege
of the powerful, but instead a subtext of anguish and frustration" (xii). On

returning to Eco's distinctions later in her text, however, Walker transforms his notion of comedy to distinguish women's and feminist productions, arguing that "female" or "women's" comedy is implicitly feminist because it, like Eco's "humor," always "undermines the law." Feminist humor, on the other hand, is "analogous to what Eco speaks of as the purely comic . . . Instead of breaking the rules, it imagines a different set of rules" (150, 151).[3]

Regina Barreca, editor of *Last Laughs: Perspectives on Women and Comedy*, presents women's comedy as having very similar general characteristics in her introduction to the volume, focusing on its subversive elements and on the reaction against oppressive conditions. She, however, uses comedy as the more inclusive term, relegating humor to "an aspect of comedy," and then redefining the comic to differentiate it from the classical model and from Eco's definition (2 no. 1). Barreca defines feminist uses of comedy as inflammatory; they seem "ultimately, not to purge desire and frustration but to transform it into action" (8). While recognizing that "the refusal to supply a happy ending" characterizes modern and postmodern work generally, not just women's comedy, Barreca (like Walker) appeals to differences between men's and women's positions in dominant cultures of discourse to argue that "the woman comic writer displays a different code of subversive thematics than her male counterparts. Her writing is characterised by the breaking of cultural and ideological frames. Her use of comedy is dislocating, anarchic and . . . unconventional" (9–10). Unlike classical comedy and more recent comedy by men, which raises questions of authority only to answer them within the boundaries of regeneration or continuation of the old law, "the woman writer forges a comedy that allows for complexity and depth without the generally oppressive didacticism so often found in the social satire of writers from Swift to Amis. The ending of comic works by women writers do not, ultimately, reproduce the expected hierarchies, or if they do it is often with a sense of dislocation even about the happiest ending" (11–12). Put more generally and working this time from feminist writers Catharine Clement and Hélène Cixous, Barreca writes that "In exploring laughter, women are exploring their own powers; they are refusing to accept social and cultural boundaries that mark the need or desire for closure as a 'universal.' Comedy is dangerous; humor is a weapon. Laughter is refusal and triumph" (14).

The comedy in our title is this comedy of social disruption and inconclusiveness, a subversively radical tool against conventional law, which nonetheless makes use of some traditional elements of the genre, comedy. By Walker's definition of women's humor and her assumption about feminist comedy, and by Barreca's definition of women's comedy, Dickinson writes that very thing in the whole range of its possibilities—sometimes subversively undermining and sometimes openly exploding the rules. She uses domestic scenes and vocabulary, overtly accepts the circumstances or conventions that her humor covertly mocks or criticizes, and manipulates stereotypes of women's roles in order to call attention to their limitations and the inequality of the system that constructs them. Dickinson's humor, like that Barreca describes in a more recent book on women's humor, "often . . . deals with those subjects traditionally reserved for tragedy: life and death, love and hate, connection and abandonment" (*Snow White* 31).

As Barreca describes in an essay in *Last Laughs*, language play can become an aggressive tool of comedy, and Dickinson makes full use of this possibility. Through metaphor and through her narrative structures, she revitalizes language that has become merely symbolic; what appears figurative is revealed to be literal (243, 244). Like the comedy Barreca outlines in her introduction, Dickinson's comic verse lacks closure and depends more on the process of saying something than on reaching a singular and definite conclusion (15, 17). The pleasure of these texts is disruptive, destabilizing instead of reassuring. While her comedy may, in Schmitz's terms, be ultimately "redemptive," it is so only to the reader or audience who can accept her levels of isolation and difference.

As important as the writer's text in comedy is the audience, the reader's or listener's necessary contribution in establishing any verbal exchange as humorous, and especially as humorous from a feminist perspective. We wish to stress this component of comedy and Dickinson's contribution to it. The extent to which one *finds* Dickinson funny, or feminist, depends on several factors. First, because much of Dickinson's comic vision stems from her gender consciousness, it is difficult to separate that consciousness, or her feminism, from her humor. To appreciate the full range of Dickinson's humor, one must be able to conceive of her as a sharp critic of her world, as a self-conscious writer identifying with (at least white middle-class) women's experience as a basis for social criticism, and as a crafter of multiple levels of intention in her poems. In contrast, to the extent that one envisions this poet as unconscious of her self and her craft, or as a victim suffering under tyrannical parents, patriarchy generally, or her own neuroses, one will not find humor in her poems. As linguist Sally McConnell-Ginet states, a double level of freeing must occur for two people to communicate (humorously or seriously) on a level subversive of normative conventions and politics. The speaker must indicate that subversion is intended—indication Dickinson provides redundantly, as many feminist critics have demonstrated. At the same time, the reader must both understand the subversive intention as possible (that is, be already familiar with it) and simultaneously accept a subversive intention as likely for the speaker—in this case, recognize the personal and cultural clues that such subversion is possible for a nineteenth-century woman writer.

The idea that the comic needs a receptive audience is familiar to writers on comedy and to comic women writers. Barreca writes about the generations that have misunderstood or misread women's comic texts, refusing to see that they are comic, overlooking the anger and criticism they contain, and seeing their choices to disrupt traditional comic structures as a failure to succeed in producing real comedy (*Last Laughs* 6–7, 17). Lisa Merrill, in her essay, "Feminist Humor: Rebellious and Self-affirming," uses philosopher Henry Bergson's claim that "our laughter is always the laughter of a group" to explain that women's "so-called 'lack of humor'" may stem from their widespread refusal to comply with the premises of male humor and from male misunderstanding or devaluation of that which women do find funny (*Last Laughs* 273). In her poem "Cascade Experiment," Alice Fulton writes that even scientific and natural-historical "truths" go unnoticed "due to bias / against such things existing." Like truths, humor appears only after we first suspect its existence.

Thus to a considerable degree, the interpreter's ability to recognize women's humor depends on presuppositions about authorial capabilities. For example, assumptions about femininity and female characteristics and what pleases, provokes, disappoints, satisfies, satiates, entices, disturbs, offends, or upsets women may prejudice readers so that women's ironic and humorous expressions are misconstrued as genuinely plaintive or earnest, or repudiated as overbearing. Both a younger contemporary of Dickinson's and Thomas Higginson provide examples of how receptions of women's humor have been routinely contained. Though John W. Burgess, an Amherst College graduate and guest at a Dickinson tea, recognized Sue Dickinson's "wit and repartee," he pronounced her "brilliant and highly cultivated" abilities "a little too sharp." Likewise, publicly praising a woman poet (Mary P. Thatcher) for her witty expression, Higginson was careful to describe it as "a good deal of *quiet* humor" (emphasis added) (Leyda 2:124, 261). Even when a woman's humor is recognized, then, it may be downplayed or dismissed as inappropriate if she is perceived as not behaving as a woman should.

The audience for Dickinson's comic performances must assume her humorous intention and share both her assumption of normative cultural frames and the ability to imagine departures from them. Up to this point we have discussed performance solely as it has to do with the intention of author and comic structural frames. Yet as a large body of literary criticism argues, performance inheres in all literary production. The dynamic relations of production between and among author, text, and readers are especially complicated. As in some modern theater and performance art, the performance of reading requires especially active participation: more than for conventional stage productions or concerts, reading demands an attentive gaze or careful ear.

Proposing definitions for uses of the term "performance," Henry Sayre writes that "in ordinary usage, a *performance* is a specific action or set of actions—dramatic, musical, athletic, and so on—which occurs on a given occasion, in a particular place" (91). Literary performances occur in the acts of both reading and writing. Since, as Hans Robert Jauss writes, "the producer is always a recipient as soon as he begins to write," the act of writing involves the performance of reading (*Question and Answer* 207). Conversely, the act of reading what Roland Barthes would call "*writerly* texts" like Dickinson's also involves the act of "writing" in that the reader must author connections across ellipses, as well as from allusions to their sources then back to the text in order to hypothesize what they mean; hence the *writerly* text aims to transform the reader from a passive consumer into a textual producer (4).

By asking readers to perform as coauthors, Dickinson creates what we might, following Alicia Ostriker, call an "open poetics" (338). Dickinson's "open poetics" are, however, far from anarchic, for Dickinson provides some leadership. For example, though her variants may offer metrical choices (i.e., different linguistic rhythms), the rhythms more or less inhere in the words among which Dickinson's readers may pick and choose. Similarly, though readers must make connections between illustrations attached to texts or between components of disjunctive metaphors, suggestions inhere in the choices offered. Long recognized as a precursor of modernism, Dickinson, in her poetic project, urges us beyond simple hierarchies between author and reader and, in doing so, beyond conventional hierarchies that organize the world. In that way, her poetic project is as democratic as Whitman's, and with him she might proclaim, "clear to me now standards not yet publish'd" ("In Paths Untrodden"). Thus the reading performances by which literature is shared involve a process of exchange that works in two directions at once (back and forth between text and reader) and are inextricably intertwined with one another.

Like "an artistic performance," a literary performance—"as opposed, for instance, to an athlete's performance or a student's performance on an examination—is further defined by its status as the single occurrence of a repeatable and preexistent text or score. Thus there is *Hamlet*, and there are its many performances; the play itself, and its interpretations" (Sayre 91). Theories of reading and performance question whether or not a literary text can exist outside its reading performances, for without readers to interpret them, poems, plays, novels, stories, essays, and epics are mere words on pages. Outside interpretation, it might be said, literature devolves to meaningless marks on the page.

Tracing developments and some inconsistencies in reader-response criticism, Jonathan Culler notes a pertinent paradox: "The more a theory stresses the reader's freedom, control, and constitutive activity, the more likely it is to lead to stories of dramatic encounters and surprises which portray reading as a process of discovery." Using the process by which a joke works as an exemplary text, he notes that "the listener is essential to the joke, for unless the listener laughs, the joke is not a joke." But "the listener does not control the outburst of laughter: the text provokes it (the joke, one says, *made me* laugh)" (72–73). Thus the dynamics of literary performance parallel the dynamics of a joke successfully delivered as both the text and the audience exercise some control.

In the "dialectic between the *intentions* of the composer or author of a work and the *interpretations* to which it is submitted by its performers" (Sayre 92), the central issue in literary study resides: who *authorizes* and controls a text's meaning? As Culler's analogy makes plain, Dickinson's productions implicitly underscore the fact that textual control—whether of the reader, the author, or the text—is dynamic and temporal. As does all humorous expression, Dickinson's witticisms, humor, and comedy accentuate the fact that there is a world outside the text, that a joke cannot just be about itself nor can it exist by itself. To be enjoyed, a joke must be performed, and performance always exceeds the formal properties of the humorous expression. Performance is in fact part of the humor, as the performance of reading is an integral part of the pleasure or effect of the text. Rhythm, rhyme (or lack thereof), condensation, metaphor, allusion, and so on are aspects of poetic structure that produce its effects, but they are not the effects themselves, for the effects occur only in the performance of reading. Similarly, the elements of a joke that produce laughter are not the elements of the laughter itself, for laughter can be enjoyed only when the joker and listener are at least under the illusion that their performances are in sync.

How distinct can anyone be from his or her performances? Richard

Poirier's interrogation of performance and its supposed separation from real life provides a useful analogy:

> Where does Nixon's fictional self-creation [or performing self] end and the historical figure begin? Can such a distinction be made about a man who watches the movie *Patton* for the third or fourth time and then orders an invasion of Cambodia meant to destroy the Viet Cong Pentagon, which he told us was there but which has never been found? (30)

Obvious from Poirier's example is the fact that performance is a *real* part of any character. Since the joke or witticism must be received to be recognized and constituted as that which it is intended to be, it cannot be distinct from its performances.

Citing Gertrude Stein and performance artists Laurie Anderson and David Antin, Sayre concludes his discussion by reflecting upon performance's transformative properties and referring to active engagements of audiences. In these terms, "performance can be defined as an activity which generates transformations, as the reintegration of art with what is 'outside' it, and 'opening up' of the 'field' " (103). Dickinson's writings are directed toward their futures with readers' responses, which are technically "outside" the originary work. Without readers, there can be no field for interpretation, thus no interpretive play by which her poetry, much less her humor, is recognized.

Though, like Sayre, we believe that performances of both speakers and readers inhere in all literary productions, our topic focuses on two more specific elements of performance. First, we propose that feminist comedy demands different particular responses from its audience than do other texts. In such comedy, the reader and the speaker must share both an assumption about the cultural norm that frames the action, and about the possibility of subversive, undermining, or explosive departures from that norm, for, as we stated earlier, feminist comedy by definition breaks away from a framing norm. Obviously, while other texts may be subversive or demand more than one type of shared assumption between reader and speaker, this is a necessary condition for feminist comedy rather than merely a sufficient one. Second, we argue that the author Dickinson deliberately creates comedic speakers in her poems, and that she clues us in to their performances through the use of theatrical gestures and props. Her speakers obviously play to audiences in ways designed to elicit amused, titillated, even shocked responses, and as a consequence, the multiple levels of performance are intentionally comic.

Comedy, at one level, is what makes us laugh—or at least smile. Comedy is funny. Although our approach to Dickinson's comedy does not focus on the kinds of humor that make one laugh or smile, Dickinson does have several outright funny poems, poems that are comic in the popular rather than the theoretical sense. Before turning to our extended and more serious discussion of comic performance in Dickinson's art, therefore, we want to provide a few examples of comic writing at the most playful end of this poet's range.[4] In these poems, Dickinson often calls attention to her speaker and her subject as "cute." She does this through a variety of techniques: through rhyme and meter, exaggeration, ludicrous images, and the genre of the animal fable. These poems are obviously contrived to charm. And yet, as the archaic definition of "cute" suggests, the cuteness is shrewd, clever. The speaker displays her ingenuousness.

In "I'm Nobody! Who are you?" for example, the speaker coyly introduces herself as charmingly unimportant. Here the poet mocks the pretensions of the public world by imagining public figures as loud bullfrogs and herself as someone unrecognizable to the crowd:

> I'm Nobody! Who are you?
> Are you – Nobody – Too?
> Then there's a pair of us!
> Don't tell! they'd advertise – you know!
>
> How dreary – to be – Somebody!
> How public – like a Frog –
> To tell one's name – the livelong June –
> To an admiring Bog!   (288)[5]

The audience who would appreciate one's announcement of self-importance has the character of a swamp, something one sinks in, not something with an opinion to be respected. Similarly, being "Somebody" in the terms of this poem constitutes self-advertisement (telling one's own name) or allowing others to "advertise" for you—that is, identity in this context is a result of staged marketing rather than of production or worth. Any person of reasonable modesty, the poet implies, would rather be hiding out with her, another "Nobody," free from the "Bog." The apparent lack of guile in the speaker's opening playfully conspiratorial tone slides into pointed—but still apparently playful—social observation, as she rhymes "Frog" with "Bog" to describe the "Somebod[ies]" and the audience she scorns. Cuteness allows the speaker to satirize her subject sharply yet keep her charm.

"She sights a Bird – she chuckles – " (507) contains similarly accessible comedy with the light ironic twist familiar in Dickinson's simplest comic poems.

> She sights a Bird – she chuckles –
> She flattens – then she crawls –
> She runs without the look of feet –
> Her eyes increase to Balls –
>
> Her Jaws stir – twitching – hungry –
> Her Teeth can hardly stand –
> She leaps, but Robin leaped the first –
> Ah, Pussy, of the Sand,
>
> The Hopes so juicy ripening –
> You almost bathed your Tongue –
> When Bliss disclosed a hundred Toes –
> And fled with every one –   (507)

In the first two stanzas, this marvelous portrait of the pouncing cat has the structure of comic suspense. The cat's motions, while described realistically enough to be immediately recognizable, exaggerate each of her movements so that the "Pussy" is cartoon-like, a figure that epitomizes hungry cat-ness. Then, with "Ah, Pussy, of the Sand," the narrative turns to provide a second and more speculative type of humor. The poet here redescribes the event in more abstract and metaphorical terms, thereby making it a kind of parable of the failed attempt to gain a prize. Rather than moralizing, however, Dickinson maintains the comic tone through her continued exaggeration, and by animating Hopes and Bliss. Just as you "almost bathe" your panting, salivating "Tongue"—the ultimate sign of animal desire—"Bliss" reveals its extraordinary mobility: it "disclose[s] a hundred Toes," "every one" carrying it safely away. Here is a comic primal scene for all failure to procure "Bliss."

As both poems above indicate, animals play major roles in Dickinson's funny poems, which often function as fables that comment on human foibles by means of the poems' furred or winged subjects. The clever jingly rhymes of many of these ditties proclaim them true forerunners of Ogden Nash.

The butterfly obtains
But little sympathy
Though favorably mentioned
In Etymology –

Because he travels freely
And wears a proper coat
The circumspect are certain
That he is dissolute –

Had he the homely scutcheon
Of modest Industry
'Twere fitter certifying
For Immortality –   (1685)

This poem opposes the New England Protestant work ethic with the sly notion that nature has more liberal values for its denizens. The butterfly, a kind of playboy of the Western skies, not only has fun but looks good—both qualities destined to make him the subject of much headshaking from the good citizens of the kind of town that Dickinson knew all too well. However, in this poem, the butterfly emerges triumphant—a candidate for Immortality by means of Etymology if not Industry. The play with all those multisyllabic rhyme words—*sympathy* with *Etymology*, *coat* with *dissolute*, and *Industry* with *Immortality*—points both to the high-minded seriousness of the town's morality and also to a means by which others outside of the system might mock it.

Dickinson writes about despised as well as admired creatures:

A Rat surrendered here
A brief career of Cheer
And Fraud and Fear.

Of Ignominy's due
Let all addicted to
Beware.

The most obliging Trap
It's tendency to snap
Cannot resist –

Temptation is the Friend
Repugnantly resigned
At last.   (1340)

If the butterfly poem questions a too-simplistic morality, this one takes an alternative stance, interrogating an equally prevalent tendency to admire the charming rogue. Not, however, because crime doesn't pay, but because, more profoundly, the excessive egotism it engenders is in the end self-defeating. The Rat, although quite properly caught, is a comic character throughout his drama because of his anarchic bravado. The jaunty meter and playful rhymes characterize him as a cocky blend of Cheer and Fraud and Fear. His problem, however, is in thinking himself bigger than his (nonexistent) britches. There is more to the world than oneself. Rats may swagger, but traps will snap. So be it.

Dickinson does not restrict her wit or whimsy to the animal kingdom. Subjects as sublime as religion or God may receive similar treatment. A brief early poem represents Dickinson in this vein:

"Faith" is a fine invention
When Gentlemen can *see* –
But *Microscopes* are prudent
In an Emergency.   (185)

Here the poet mocks several aspects of conventional religious belief with a very light touch. Like the microscope, "Faith" is an invention, presumably designed for its usefulness. Indeed, she tells us, it is a "fine" invention, her quotation marks around the word itself providing only the slightest hint that what is called "Faith" may not be identical with the speaker's own definition of the word. And then the more pointed qualifications begin. Faith is fine—for "Gentlemen" already blessed with sight, when they are without immediate problems. In a state of emergency (presumably the natural state of all those who are not gentlemen or without confidence in their native vision), it is best to keep a more practical invention handy. In the role of sage counselor advising her charges to prepare wisely for their future, Dickinson here compares an element of belief basic to the history and conventions of New England to any other product marking the progress of knowledge; best to trust to science for clear vision if you don't start out with a lot going for you already, or if times get rough.

Dickinson is as willing to take on literary brahmins as she is to satirize "Faith" in her comic verse. For example, her "I taste a liquor never brewed – " has long been recognized as a witty poetic response to Emerson's "Bacchus":

> I taste a liquor never brewed —
> From Tankards scooped in Pearl –
> Not all the Vats upon the Rhine
> Yield such an Alcohol!
>
> Inebriate of Air – am I –
> And Debauchee of Dew –
> Reeling – thro endless summer days ,
> From inns of Molten Blue –
>
> When "Landlords" turn the drunken Bee
> Out of the Foxglove's door –
> When Butterflies – renounce their "drams" ,
> I shall but drink the more!
>
> Till Seraphs swing their snowy Hats ,
> And Saints – to windows run –
> To see the little Tippler
> Leaning against the – Sun –   (214, using variant lines)

Pointedly comic, Dickinson's rapid rhythms, glittering images, and exaggerated depictions recycle representations of the exotic, the quotidian, and the holy to portray the Poet's creative mind. Like Emerson's, her poem draws on the analogy likening poetic vision to the state of intoxication. But while Emerson elevates his view by allying it with Greek mythology, Dickinson's tippler smirks at the mythic and the sacred, deflating pretentious characterizations of poets' endeavors. Yet she does this not in a scoffing or belittling way, but with charming, delightful description. Both poems move from a preoccupation with the mystical to a focus on the diminutive and earthbound and then conclude with cosmic, heavenly imagery; Emerson's poem, however, is very sober and serious, while Dickinson's is comic, as revealed in the alliteration in "Debauchee of Dew" and "Seraphs swing their snowy Hats" and in likening a flower to a tavern and a bee to a customer. While "tippler" connotes a dizzy, gleeful spirit as well as a local character who savors his or her cocktails, "reeling" brings to mind a lively country dance and implies a state of vertigo not relieved by the lyric's end: the "I" is, in the final line, "Leaning," not standing upright. Significantly, while Emerson writes of "dancing Pleiads and eternal men" as if he enjoys some union or kinship with them, Dickinson's speaker does not join the heavenly inhabitants, or seraphs, but grins from a distance, amazing them and the saints with her drunken reverie. The "Saints," or eternal men of her poem, are entrapped behind windows while the speaker travels at liberty, resting when and where she pleases. Her speaker even asserts a kind of superiority to the angels, for she leans, unscathed, against the sun which would melt their "snowy Hats," dissolving and then evaporating them. The idea of heavenly, presumably comfortable inhabitants donning hats made of an earthly, chilly substance is enticingly ridiculous.

Such carefree representation of the age-old comparison between poets and inebriates is sure to amuse, but it also realigns conventional hierarchies so that the element of fun is less likely to be regarded as trivial than as vital. Part of Dickinson's poetic charm is that she elevates the ostensibly trivial to importance, frequently finding fun where the rest of us would do little more than take for granted. Of the most ephemeral of plants, she writes:

> The Mushroom
> is the Elf of
> Plants –
> At Evening, it
> is not –
> At Morning, in
> a Truffled Hut
> It stop upon
> a Spot
>
> As if it tarried
> always
> And yet its'
> whole Career
> Is shorter than
> a Snake's
> Delay –
> And fleeter than
> a Tare –
>
> 'Tis Vegetation's
> Juggler –

The Germ of
Alibi –
Doth like a
Bubble antedate
And like a
Bubble, hie –

I feel as if
the Grass was
pleased
To have it
intermit ,
This Surreptitious
Scion
Of Summer's
circumspect.

Had Nature
Any Supple Face
Or could
she one
contemn –
Had Nature
an Apostate –
That Mushroom ,
it is Him!   (Set 13; 1298)

The tiniest, apparently most negligible food grows as if it will last forever.
Dickinson's most frolicsome clause, "It stop upon / a Spot," emphasizes the
point immediately following: time seems irrelevant to these plants whose
ephemerality, like that of bubbles, is essence and taken for granted; though
each is shortlived, the mushroom as plant can be reproduced time and
again. In the version left among the sets and fascicles in her drawer,
"Stop" is written precisely above "Spot," and ends the first verse. Not
only do the letter inversions evince Dickinson's romp with the various
ways words look and sound with only the slightest of changes, but the
monosyllabic assonance slows the poem's rhythm, and even teases, "As if
it" might tarry "always." "Hut" creates for the preposition "in" the possibility of meaning "into" and so animates the personification: the mushroom is not just standing there in human dress, but, walking around, steps
into a hut and stops. Through cartoon-like depiction, Dickinson jauntily

exhorts and shows readers how to take pleasure in the mundane. Of traditional distinctions between "high" and "low," frivolous and sublime, then, we can never be too sure. Alluringly, Dickinson's speaker urges readers to adore every nuance of the natural world and suggests that having fun is not simply fribble.

Dickinson's poetry is profoundly humorous; at times whimsical and witty, it is throughout imbued with the spirit and form of comedy. This book approaches the shape and significance of that comedy by examining three of its central modes: tease, cartooning, and excess or grotesquerie. In the following chapters, each of us independently explores one of these arenas of Dickinson's humor. Not surprisingly, we move in different directions in these chapters, at times disagreeing over precise delineations of a common claim. Nonetheless, the argument of this chapter about the importance of the interplay of gender and audience in both the production and reception of Dickinson's humor remains key to all that follows. By providing our readers with our individual as well as our collaborative arguments, we hope to stimulate yet further work in and more diverse approaches to this very rich field.

In Chapter 2, "The Big Tease," Suzanne Juhasz argues that tease is a matter of voice, of tone. Tease pokes fun, provokes, and disentangles; it also lures and allures—or flirts. It is a do and don't signal, both defense and offense. Tease is Dickinson's response to patriarchal power as it both attracts and angers her. "The Big Tease" shows how Dickinson challenges social situations, both general and personal, by teasing.

Juhasz explores two interrelated ways in which Dickinson teases. Tease that pokes fun, provokes, and/or disentangles is a response to the privileged definitions for cultural norms upon which patriarchy is based. The provocation of this form of joking works to disentangle such definitions from their accustomed contexts, thereby presenting not only a different perspective or point of view toward that definition but in the process raising the crucial issue of definitional reliability. By providing another way to see it, one that pokes fun at and deliberately undermines a culturally sanctioned definition, Dickinson causes the very normativeness of that definition to become suspect—and adjustable.

Another meaning of tease which characterizes Dickinson's linguistic performances is to play on and with another's desire. If Dickinson teases the subject of a poem by provoking or critiquing, she teases her audience—both singular (the "you" of a poem's direct address) and plural (the "you" of the reader) by means of charm. To tease is to promise but not deliver, and its sexual implications—striptease, come-on—cannnot be overlooked. Tease is this woman's response to male power and authority, a challenge consisting not of direct attack but of allure. Sexuality is power, but only when you don't submit—especially with regard to the fathers who symbolize male power. Fathers are both attractive and dangerous; tease is safe as well as provocative.

Dickinson's poems tease the reader as well as their subjects. If only because readers are also part of the patriarchal society, our desire for Dickinson and her poem is justifiably suspect. Her poems consistently promise but do not completely deliver, inviting our participation precisely because they will not reveal all. In this way they protect her even as they present her. Yet the presentation, the performance, is as much a part of the tease as is the withholding. Tease creates the space of the poem, positioned between the mind of the poet and the culture she questions.

Like her teasing strategies, Dickinson's cartooning is deeply imbedded in the cultural life she questions. As Martha Nell Smith argues in Chapter 3, sending flowers, fruit, and baked goods to neighbors was as customary in Amherst middle-class society as the daily exchanges of gossip down at the post office, over the fence, or in parlors, and through comic descriptions Dickinson made "cartoons" out of these commonplace occasions. For example, when she sent a basket of berries to Mrs. Henry Hills, wife of a local manufacturer of straw hats, she labeled the outside "Babes in the Woods" (L 615, 1879?). In another letter, satirically characterizing both her own participation in local gossip and others' receptions to a young woman speaking her mind, Dickinson relates a bit of parlor gossip to brother Austin:

> We had a very pleasant visit from the Monson folks—they came one noon and stayed till the next. They agree beautifully with Father on the "present generation." They decided that they hoped every young man who smoked would take fire. I respectfully intimated that I thought the result would be a vast conflagration, but was instantly put down. (L 123)

In both of these examples—the merry note attached to a simple gift of berries, the wry commentary on her elders—Dickinson transforms neighborly and familial rituals into delightful entertainment. Though these particular "cartoons" are limited in scope and to a particular occasion, in her chapter Smith contends that Dickinson's cartooning was far from provincial, ranged widely in subject, and launched ambitious sociopolitical critiques.

"The Poet as Cartoonist" is a tripartite discussion investigating several ways in which Dickinson may be said to be "cartooning." In the chapter's first section, Smith defines cartoons and cartooning and situates Dickinson's productions both in her immediate culture and in light of how works with such popular appeal have traditionally been devalued as art. The second section presents three of Dickinson's layouts and one drawing that challenge contemporary institutions. In such visual cartoons, Dickinson calls five types of cultural authority into question: that of poetic tradition, that of patriotism, that of romantic thralldom, that of the patriarchal family, and that established by the rigidities of the printing press. In the third section, Smith critiques several of Dickinson's language "cartoons," epistolary and lyric. The epistolary cartoons range from cheery cards for her nephew to notes to her cousins poking good-natured fun at a particularly prim aunt. On the perpetually monumental topics of death and sex, the poetic cartoons work serially, with individual stanzas suggesting stories in ways similar to the way the panels of a cartoon strip set a narrative into motion. All of the examinations reveal Dickinson's irreverent interrogations and her implicit exhortations to subsequent readers about the importance of active, energetic, playful reading.

In Chapter 4, Cristanne Miller discusses that excess or grotesquerie which adheres in the language or imagery of a poem, although it may also appear in the narrative. "The Humor of Excess" turns to Dickinson's poems that contain moments of wildness or irrationality or an extremity of metaphor that takes one beyond the bounds of common sense, or apparent coherence, or even good taste. Such excess often takes the form of grotesquerie; the speaker may present the human body in distorted forms, or surreal representations of extreme emotion—sometimes joyful but more often of pain. These are the poems in which Dickinson seems closest to losing control, perhaps because they are about loss of control, the rush toward chaos that occurs at moments of great intensity. Like Sappho, however, Dickinson details these moments of chaos or grotesquerie or— as Miller calls it more generally—excess with such precision and detail that one is forced to recognize the separation of author from speaker, or the element of drama, of performance, involved in the representation of the narrative.

Miller argues that these may be the poems in which Dickinson's art is most on display, because their very extremity both tricks the reader into thinking that the speaker's experience could not be imagined ("who could make up such pain?") and therefore that the poet and speaker must be identical, at the same time that the extremity creates a kind of humor because of its egregious unreality. Humor, in these poems, does not reside in cuteness, or a teasing play, or in a structural resemblance to cartoon visuals and narratives but rather simply in the fact that the poet's language or images go too far to be taken completely seriously. As the phrasing above suggests, "completely" is the operative word here. These poems of excess are on the one hand not funny at all, are indeed among Dickinson's most terrible, darkest poetic expressions. On the other hand, to the extent that the reader interprets the language and metaphors of these poems literally, attempting actually to imagine what she describes, the horror crosses that peculiar psychological line where it becomes funny, or at least humorous. Like the canvases of Salvador Dali or other anti-realistic painters, these poems present a landscape so out of this world that one is simultaneously, or alternately, amused and appalled.

Such excess may stem from a variety of causes, not least among them an exuberance of imagination and a delight in exploiting conventions that reveal themselves in several other elements of Dickinson's poetics. The grotesquerie of this excess, however, and the focus of much of the excess on physical experience, often implicitly gendered as female, suggests that it may also constitute an explosive response to the poet's sense of suffocation by social conventions. Like carnivalesque escape from the constraints of everyday behavior, the display of these poems may mark the poet's desire to at least briefly experience chaos as a release from the boundaries of ordinary living. Miller uses the anachronistic analogy of twentieth-century camp production to explore this rebellious aspect of display, with its sexual and gendered innuendos, in Dickinson's poems of excess.

As a whole, *Comic Power in Emily Dickinson* argues that Dickinson's comic vision destabilizes, subverts, and reimagines cultural situations. As we discuss in our final chapter, the poem becomes a space for transformation, because it is the place for questioning the external world and even rearranging it. First, by transforming the relationship between the reader and the text, Dickinson creates the conditions for a more dynamic and unstructured or open reading experience. The text becomes a field for volatile appropriation in the most physical and positive sense. At the same time, the poem is as guarded as it is beckoning. Because Dickinson cannot count on getting the friendly and adventurous reader she desires, she creates defensive structures that in turn force the reader to take responsibility for textual meaning. Once she has established such a literary environment, the poem becomes available for a transforming vision of the world. For Dickinson this means not creating a brand-new fantasy but disassembling and rearranging, in ways that radically reshape them, the conventions and structures with which she lives every day. As we discuss in the chapters that follow, this strategy takes the most literal and the most metaphoric of forms.

Chapter 2
The Big Tease

by Suzanne Juhasz

I

They wont frown always – some sweet Day
When I forget to teaze –
They'll recollect how cold I looked
And how I just said "Please."

Then They will hasten to the Door
To call the little Girl
Who cannot thank Them for the Ice
That filled the lisping full.   (874)

THUS DICKINSON, speaking in the persona of a little girl, takes her revenge on adults who, in their imposition of the culture's definitions of good-little-girl-hood, have tried to suppress her vitality while she was still alive. In response, she tries to evoke their guilt by portraying herself as really dead; then you'll be sorry, she warns. In her first stanza, the act of teasing is contrasted to that of saying please. If saying please is the sign of a proper little girl, this one achieves that distinction only on her deathbed. In life, as the second stanza continues to intimate, this child was a bit more loquacious, outspoken. For example, she liked to tease. Now, in death, her voice is stilled in a macabre transformation of a typical summer afternoon, when a child might have asked for a little ice on which to suck, to cool her. She is really cold now, she is dead now, and that ice becomes an image of murderous import, a sign of the adults' attempts to silence her.

Not only does the poem talk about teasing, it is a tease. The speaker is playing at being dead, and the poet is playing at being a little girl. Dickinson uses a little girl speaker as a vantage point for raising issues about female socialization, and she asks that speaker to take a particularly teasing stance toward the adults who are the most immediate implied audience for her words. Teasing, because she goads and baits them with her picture of an untimely death. She does not challenge or threaten them outright but implies her critique through her little fiction, the image of the ice-filled mouth. Teasing, because the very picture of silence she creates is undermined (or teased) by the way it is achieved through skillful speech. If her deathbed vision requires the suppression of teasing, teasing's profound importance is demonstrated by the poem that has created such a vision.

Tease is habitually Dickinson's response to patriarchal power, something that simultaneously attracts, angers, and frequently frightens her. With tease rather than with direct attack, Dickinson questions and negotiates power relationships as they are traditionally structured in terms of hierarchies and dominance. Teasing is defense as well as invitation, and it provides a space—in Dickinson's case, the space is the poem—in which renegotiation as well as critique is possible.

Dickinson teases in several related ways. Tease that pokes fun, provokes, and/or disentangles is targeted at the privileged definitions for cultural norms upon which patriarchy is based. The provocation of her joking works to disentangle definitions from their accustomed contexts, thereby presenting not only a different perspective or point of view toward that definition but in the process raising the crucial issue of definitional reliability, questioning the fact of cultural orthodoxy. By providing another way to see it, one that pokes fun at and deliberately undermines a culturally sanctioned definition, Dickinson causes the very normativeness of that definition to become suspect—and adjustable. Suddenly the world has been redefined: what's down could be up, what's out could be in.

This "world" to which I refer now is the world of the poem. The real or external world may be what is under scrutiny, but the changes occur in the space of the poem. Positioned between the mind of the poet and the culture she inhabits, the poem's space is where she can challenge dominance and hegemony. The space of the poem is not exactly safe—someone could, after all, read it; but it is the best and only place Dickinson knows for taking the chance, for making a try. Consequently, if we understand Dickinson as a comic writer, what we mean is that the world of the poem, in its contiguous relation to the culture itself, is the space where cultural codes are not only cast into doubt but rearranged. The notion of comedy as subversive social criticism that breaks cultural and ideological frames is amplified by its transformational possibilities, its project, in Neil Schmitz' words, "to confront the sad pull of gravity, the doomsward movement of rushing time, and transform the feeling of it" (7). Especially as the comic is located in language, validating language's power to create alternative spaces, alternative worlds, the life that is affirmed is a life realized through and by means of language.

If Dickinson teases her subject by provoking or critiquing, by disentangling definition from accustomed meaning, she teases her audience—both singular (the "you" of a poem's direct address) and plural (the "you" of her readers)—by means of charm. Here Dickinson teases by playing on and with another's desire, attracting or luring but not delivering—i.e., flirting. The sexual implications of this kind of tease cannot be overlooked. Images of striptease come to mind; visions of the poem as "come-on." The performance of tease is the response of a woman poet to a male-dominated society. Dickinson identifies power and authority with maleness. Why should she not, when almost everything and everyone who possessed it in her experience, from father to teacher to editor to God, was male? Further, "all men" had power over her. To challenge that power was not such a simple matter as to take it from them, in something like hand-to-hand combat. That is what sons do. Dickinson was a daughter, and daughters flirt. They use the so-called power that the culture assigns to them, their sexuality, to allure and to lure. But they don't give in, or put out, because sexuality is power only when you don't submit—especially with regard to fathers. Fathers are dangerous as well as attractive; tease is safe as well as provocative. A do and don't signal, it is both defense and offense.

Dickinson's poems tease the reader as well as the direct objects of their address.[1] If only because readers are also part of the patriarchal society, our desire for Dickinson and her poem is justifiably suspect. Our desire is to know and to possess. Her words attract us, and we want to know what they mean; we want her words to lead us to her. However, both Dickinson and her words promise but do not deliver. Thus the poem becomes the space between the arousal of desire and its fulfillment. Teasing creates gaps—lacunae between images and words. It's all done with mirrors, or lights—the flash between what you see and what you don't (between what you want to see and what you think you see). Tease invites participation precisely because it will not reveal all. In these gaps we, the audience, insert ourselves, so that any satisfaction we experience comes as much from what we have put there as from what she has suggested. As Karl Keller notes, "the lure is alluring and also a little cruel. The tease—spidery—attracts, overwhelms, and then abandons. She wins you and then will not have you even when she needs you. You are on your own, happy victim, with the lovely web, the poem" (72).

Dickinson's tease works, as Umberto Eco notes, "in the interstices between narrative and discursive structures" ("The Frames of Comic Freedom" 8). It isn't the story, it's the way it's told. Tease is a matter of voice, of intonation and emphasis. It isn't the grammar or syntax, but the pauses, the hesitations, the breaks in the sentence structure. Poems tease on several levels of discourse. Through their argument they tease their subjects; through their stance they tease their audience. Tease is clearly a performance, and Dickinson has in her repertoire a range of characters that she plays, each of whom is in some way looking in from the peripheries of culture. Small animals and insects, provincial hicks, and little girls all offer a skewed perspective for redefining experience such that familiar norms and values become suspect. Yet Dickinson's most powerful teaser is the character of the woman poet, who uses her very difference—from conventional women, from conventional men—to attract the interest of just such ordinary folks so that she can at the very least undermine their most cherished assumptions.

In Chapter 1, in our look at some of Dickinson's funny poems, we show how Dickinson's furred and winged subjects come to us in little fables which critique society, as fables do, by contrasting it with the ways of nature. In many of these lighthearted verses, the narrator identifies with the more "natural" point of view of the animals and therewith questions social norms. This idea of "natural" becomes "innocence" when it characterizes the speaker herself, and the ingenue becomes one of Dickinson's favorite teasers. Neil Schmitz begins his examination of "Huckspeech"— the voice of Huckleberry Finn—by noting the function of such a voice. "It signifies . . . the almost-voice of an almost-child, wary innocence, an almost-innocence . . . the speech of the illiterate, the speech of the preliterate, of the poor, and of children . . . the excluded language of the vulnerable, the ignorant, the innocent" (96–97). The perspective of ingenuousness in Dickinson's poetry is a tease from the word go, because it is a role assumed by an educated, adult, cultured woman. It is a way to play at innocence, to imagine a condition beyond the full constraints of culture, and then to use it as a position from which to critique the culture. A sophisticated person pretends to be an unsophisticated person in order to make a sophisticated point.

Dickinson's provincial hicks are one version of the ingenue role. They are a place to begin, to watch how Dickinson teases her world. For example, when Dickinson announces that she sees "New Englandly," it is to take on all manner of orthodoxies that are as uncomfortable to her speaker as stiff corsets and high-heeled shoes.

The Robin's my Criterion for Tune –
Because I grow – where Robins do –
But, were I Cuckoo born –

I'd swear by him –
The ode familiar – rules the Noon –
The Buttercup's, my whim for Bloom –
Because, we're Orchard sprung –
But were I Britain born,
I'd Daisies spurn –
None but the Nut – October fit –
Because, through dropping it,
The Seasons flit – I'm taught –
Without the Snow's Tableau
Winter, were lie – to me –
Because I see – New Englandly –
The Queen, discerns like me –
Provincially –   (285)

Orchard sprung, this speaker pits her avowedly provincial point of view against all of the orthodoxies she can imagine. She is staunchly republican, just like her colonial ancestors, and in assigning legitimate reality to things American as opposed to British, she likewise uses concrete details to question the domination of the abstract, particular examples to query the authority of the general. In short, in this poem all hegemonic power is suspect, from monarchies to literary canons.

The teasing tone is most obvious in the poem's conclusion, that tongue-in-cheek but clearly rebellious remark: "The Queen, discerns like me – / Provincially – ." But the poem's tease begins right at the beginning, with its riddling mode. Riddle asks us to rethink comfortable assumptions in order to find an answer that was there all along, except that those assumptions got in the way of our seeing it.[2] What is black and white and red all over? How can a robin be a criterion? The opening line juxtaposes concrete against abstract, "Robin" against "Tune," setting the stage for a poem that privileges experience as opposed to theory. In fact, this particular riddle can be answered only if the personal experience, and perspective, of its speaker is understood and validated. The second line identifies her alternate point of view: "Because I grow – where Robins do – ." This is someone whose teaching comes from what she knows with her senses, sees outside her own door. Just a local yokel, sitting in her garden, listening to the robins sing. Yet even as she asks us to take her kind of word for it, her very project lets us in on the further intricacies of the tease. To juxtapose the standards of life against the standards of poetry, as in "The ode familiar," is to be a poetically sophisticated yokel, who will put her robin up against Keats' nightingale any day. The perspective of the hick is clearly an orchestrated stance deliberately undertaken to tease out alternative attitudes about reality.

Whim rather than vested authority rules the Noon; that is, individual and personal experience takes the place of unilateral truth. The speaker is pointedly American, pointedly countrified, opposing her orchard classroom against British book learning. Here in America, we may read odes to nightingales, but we hear the robin's voice—and make our poems from it. Experience is thus relativized, depending upon the continent in which it happens. As lines 5–9 go on to maintain, in the matter of bloom, or beauty, the American poet uses buttercup, daisy, or clover as criterion (Dickinson's alternate for "Daisies spurn" in line 9 is "Clovers – scorn – "); on the other hand, were she "Britain born," she'd probably think in terms of primroses.

The poem continues on with its seasonal lessons, through the acorns of October to the snowstorms of winter. "No ideas but in things," as a subsequent American poet, William Carlos Williams, was to say. Dickinson privileges "things" always to point out their relation to authority and to truth. "Without the Snow's Tableau / Winter, were lie – to me – ." The concept "Winter" is not valid, that is, without the experience, snow. The abstract requires the concrete to be true; and concretes differ. If winter equals snow for a New Englander, it does not for a New Zealander. To see New Englandly is thus an axiom for the local and the ingenuous perspective that will not bow to generalized definitions for cultural norms, because it will not acknowledge their power. It is a validation of everyone's essential provinciality.

"The Queen, discerns like me – / Provincially – ." A cat, or in this case, a New England hick, can not only look at a queen but have equal authority. Nor can there be—it is the same thing—one, and only one, language to reify truth. Seeing New Englandly means taking local, personal, "familiar," experiential knowledge and basing language usage on it. Consequently, an American poet can be someone who spent only a term at a ladies' seminary, a woman who lives at home. In this way Dickinson's provincial poet not only teases all that is traditionally canonical, from the inherited power of royalty to the supremacy of English verse to the authority of abstract language, but teases a reader's own belief in any of these guiding principles. How can a robin be a criterion? If a New England poet says so, and if you, as reader, accept the perspective that the poem creates. If you have been teased into seeing New Englandly, then you have entered into a new world—the America of Dickinson's poem.

The voice of ingenuousness is clearly a performance, a character created before our eyes by a poet who plays upon the contrast she establishes between the speaker and the culture that is called into question. Dickinson's New England rustic is a voice that she likes to use to interrogate issues of class and power.

> I'm saying every day
> "If I should be a Queen, tomorrow" –
> I'd do this way –
> And so I deck, a little,
>
> If it be, I wake a Bourbon,
> None on me, bend supercilious –
> With "This was she –
> Begged in the Market place –
> Yesterday."
>
> Court is a stately place –
> I've heard men say –
> So I loop my apron, against the Majesty
> With bright Pins of Buttercup –
> That not too plain –
> Rank – overtake me –
>
> And perch my Tongue
> On Twigs of singing – rather high –
> But this, might be my brief Term
> To qualify –
>
> Put from my simple speech all plain word –
> Take all other accents, as such I heard
> Though but for the Cricket – just,
> And but for the Bee –
> Not in all the Meadow –
> One accost me –
>
> Better to be ready –
> Than did next morn
> Meet me in Aragon –
> My old Gown – on –

And the surprised Air
Rustics – wear –
Summoned – unexpectedly –
To Exeter – (373)

This speaker is like a rural Eliza Doolittle, a little flower girl with delusions of grandeur. Unlike the speaker in "The Robin's my Criterion for Tune – ," this girl isn't questioning the queen's authority: not explicitly. But the poem does it for her, or rather, through her. Her monologue demonstrates how the speaker's "barefoot rank" is intensified, not nullified, by her desire for the royal life; in the process, it is shown to be a "royalty" of a different sort. Once again, absolutism is replaced by a relativism underscored by democratic principles. The intricate multiplicity of the performance is a constant tease: the beggar girl pretends to be a queen and in the process validates the beauty in her "lowly" existence—as written by a woman who was herself not a servant but a member of the aristocracy of a country town. Thus class identity keeps shifting in shape and meaning before us.

The speaker of the poem lives, she tells us, in a double world: against her everyday experience she poses the possibility of change: "'If I should be a Queen, tomorrow' – ." To prepare for that eventuality, however, she alters her everyday, every day: she "decks." Her narrative may be ingenuous, but it is hardly simple, as what she hypothesizes participates in her reality, for her ideas about rank alter not only her status as "beggar" but our own ideas about what royalty means.

Her plan is to be prepared, so that when the call comes, she will already be transformed; then no one will be able to remember that only yesterday she was a beggar girl. Therefore, when she says, "If it be, I wake a Bourbon," we cannot really tell whether the call she awaits comes from outside or inside of her. She may wake a Bourbon because she has made herself one. In this poem, "Bourbon," "Aragon," and "Exeter" seem less signifiers for external place and position than of a state of mind.[3]

However, her changes underline rather than alter her provinciality; she may be transformed, but not into the foreigner of her fantasy. The alterations she brings about in her appearance and in her voice make her more, not less, countrified. More essentially, rather than superficially, rural. Against the possibility of majesty she adorns herself with "Pins of Buttercup": her gold is natural, not the product of a jeweler; free, not costly. At the same time, she tries to affect an upper-class tone, but her very metaphors for this process, "perch my Tongue / On Twigs of singing," reveal her essential connection with the meadow, not the courts. Thus, although she fancifies her vocabulary and her accent, at least some of the denizens in her particular meadow, the cricket and the bee, see through her disguise and "accost" her for it. At heart, she is, like the bird who signifies poet in so many of Dickinson's poems, a self-taught, "natural" singer.

In her fantasy of royalty she makes herself ready for the moment when she will find herself at court, in Aragon or Exeter. She imagines that, decked as she is—no old gown or surprised air for her—they will take her as already one of their own. However, the effect of her discourse on her readers is exactly the opposite. She proves herself to be no bumpkin, even if she is of the country, not because she is a soul-mate to the gentrified but because she isn't. Her self-creation of royalty has intensified her difference from, not similarity to, foreign aristocratic ideals, making her not so much naïve and foolish (imagine thinking a buttercup would take the place of a brooch of gold) as queenly in another way: first lady of the meadow where she already lives.

Dickinson's creation of this little beggar girl seems less a study in the dramatic monologue than a representation of one aspect of her own complicated psyche. True, in social class she ranks among the Amherst upper crust; but as a woman she holds second-class citizenship, and among the royalty of poets she is unknown and lowly. Except, as she tells us in poem 326, "among" her mind, where she, like her poem's speaker, decks; "It's full as Opera – ." Even as the beggar girl unsettles our ideas about what constitutes royalty by creating a version of it that is both different from the norm and essentially private, so the poem, like "The Robin's my Criterion for Tune – ," asks us to think about standards in poetry and the place of the self-taught, self-created, woman poet.

The ingenue is the perfect role for the tease of the outsider. It plays on the experience of exclusion to invoke knowledge that is present but unacknowledged. As Neil Schmitz suggests, "It is emotionally rite and socially rong" (97). As a consequence, this voice can tempt us into seeing from the other side. This is why Dickinson uses the voice of the little girl so often. It can sound like one thing and reveal something else. It can sound innocent and reveal experience, as Blake, too, had understood. It can sound like goodness and reveal badness; sound like badness and reveal goodness. It superimposes moral values like goodness and badness over gender characteristics, so that we have to question our understanding of all of these attributes and their relation to one another.

Dickinson's child persona is frequently a naughty little girl. Part of the attraction of this role for her is that it is less directly threatening than an adult voice, permitting her, as Barbara Mossberg has so persuasively

argued, to get away with being bad.[4] At the same time, however, the voice
of that bad little girl, flouting the pressures of acculturation, is seductive
because it cannot help but speak through the trappings or wrappings of
the (good) little girl. What I mean is that little girls are by definition good;
good is a part of the cultural definition of girl. "Good" in girl terms means
cute, quiet, trivial. A bad little girl is a contradiction in terms. Badness
does not make of her a boy, but a non-girl. A perverse outsider does not
turn into an insider but a deconstructed outsider, alluring just because of
the now-you-see-it, now-you-don't quality of her come-on. This kind of
tease can bring out all manner of contradictions in situations apparently
clearcut, simple, and secure.

The oft-quoted poem 251 is a good place to see the bad little girl in
action.

> Over the fence –
> Strawberries – grow –
> Over the fence –
> I could climb – if I tried, I know –
> Berries are nice!
>
> But – if I stained my Apron –
> God would certainly scold!
> Oh, dear, – I guess if He were a Boy –
> He'd – climb – if He could!   (251)

Here is the ingenuous child: "Berries are nice!" Here is the good little
girl, worried about being scolded, "Oh, dear." Here is the bad little girl,
speaking out of turn and struggling to get free: "I could climb – if I tried,
I know." Here is the accumulation of centuries of gender socialization:
"But – if I stained my Apron – / God would certainly scold!" Good girls
don't climb fences of any sort, and they don't get any kind of dirt on them.

The tease culminates in the final couplet: "I guess if He were a Boy – /
He'd climb – if He could!" The emphasis on these lines can go either on
He or on Boy. If we stress the word "He," we get a contrast between
adulthood and childhood. God's adulthood, so distanced and tame, is
poised against the possibility of an adventuresome boyhood. As adult, He
has forgotten or ignored the reality of those for whom he makes the rules.
But if we stress "Boy," the speaker's gendered distance from her God becomes stronger yet. God may once have been a boy (a climber), but this
speaker is clearly a girl. Her boyish desire to climb, therefore, makes her
a bad girl because she would make a good boy. She is prohibited from her

natural bent by gender rules that inhibit childish behavior in girls, who
are therefore negated as children as well as adults. As Mossberg argues,
"Her assumption is that God has a double standard for boys and girls—
not unlike her father and society in general" (118). How could a God, who
thus doubly denies her inclinations, be her spiritual father? His very rules
make her an altogether different species: entirely marginal.

> I never felt at Home – Below –
> And in the Handsome Skies
> I shall not feel at Home – I know –
> I dont like Paradise –
>
> Because it's Sunday – all the time –
> And Recess – never comes –
> And Eden'll be so lonesome
> Bright Wednesday Afternoons –
>
> If God could make a visit –
> Or ever took a Nap –
> So not to see us – but they say
> Himself – a Telescope
>
> Perennial beholds us –
> Myself would run away
> From Him – and Holy Ghost – and All –
> But there's the "Judgment Day"!   (413)

In this poem we watch the voice of innocence trying to get away with
criticism which would be labeled heretical in a more mature-sounding
evaluation: "I don't like Paradise." But we see as well the tension between
such innocence and the poet who writes that way; for if the child speaker
is guileless enough to think she can get away with her verbal rebellion, the
poet is aware of its potential repercussions. As Mossberg writes, "In a
strategy used by science-fiction writers and satirists, Dickinson projects
the future in order to criticize the present and the past" (120). Do poems
exist in a free space, a peephole on the culture but not really a part of it?
Or are there reverberations and consequences for language acts? If so, the
poem has to be careful, it has to cover its tracks; the poet herself may have
to protect the little girl from the possibilities of a spanking, or worse.

"I never felt at Home – Below – ," she begins. This is a very naughty
little girl, who pertly announces her disaffection with her culture. But she

is as well a sad and lonely little girl, who has experienced the rejection that her difference from traditional femaleness has already occasioned. Such a child longs all the more for some other source for home; but the only other place of which she can think that isn't her world, Paradise, doesn't seem a candidate, either—no matter the allusions to "home" that litter all the hymns she knows. As Jane Eberwein writes, "Obviously Amherst is no paradise for a timid child, nor has it conditioned her to anticipate boundless love and joy" (235). Her reasons, as she enumerates them, turn into a critique of a religious doctrine patently patriarchal, because it is just like life with father on earth, only worse. Sunday all the time: nothing but church in the morning and being closed up with the family for the rest of the day; never playing and never going outside. The lonesomeness of Eden on bright Wednesday afternoons seems to have more to do with the loss of the out-of-doors than of any particular playmates. Consequently, nature, not culture, emerges as the only place where a person who is different can go. Paradise is just society raised to its nth degree. The scrutiny of her own father, surely worst of all on Sundays, when he is home for so much longer, is exaggerated in her portrait of a God who is one unblinking eyeball—never going away, never even sleeping, "a Telescope / Perennial"!

Given the scope of the problem outlined here, the typical child's solution, running away from home, seems pointless, even to the child herself. Where could she run to? Even nature is implicated in the final result of "Him – and Holy Ghost – and All – ": the Judgment Day. Her need to rebel does not discount the overwhelming power of the system where she cannot find a home. Consequently, the naughtiness in the poem—it's both cute and titillating to disrupt our belief in a loving father—is undercut by its loneliness, the fate of a daughter who understands the paucity of love that she has known. The pain of the child speaker is amplified by the adult knowledge of the poet, who has undergone it for so much longer. The poet has run away to the poem, a vantage-point for firing off volleys at the world that has hurt her. But what about the Judgment Day? If God's telescopic eye reads the poem as well as everything else, how can the poem be safe? Only if God sees its naughtiness as cute and consequently, harmless. If he chuckles when the little girl stamps her foot and just tweaks her pigtails. The posture of the bad little girl is a tease, therefore, a performance that protects the deeper anger and alienation that it reveals.

The following example of graveyard humor demonstrates yet again the implicit tease in the tension between innocence and experience that the child voice creates.

We do not play on Graves –
Because there is'nt Room –
Besides – it is'nt even – it slants
And People come –

And put a Flower on it –
And hang their faces so –
We're fearing that their Hearts will drop –
And crush our pretty play –

And so we move as far
As Enemies – away –
Just looking round to see how far
It is – Occasionally –   (467)

The voice of ingenuousness has the prerogative of taking things literally, at face value. From the perspective of someone who is "only" a child,
graves make a fine place to play—except maybe that they're a little small,
with a tendency to slant; what's worse, people are always coming around
and bothering you there. What would be the matter with a nice grave in
a quiet churchyard, except that grownups treat them in this peculiar sort
of way, bringing to them an oppressive burden of unhappiness? From the
child's perspective, the grave is a stone; it is adults who invest it with
solemn meanings and portentous symbolism.

The change in the tone of the final stanza is a response to and articulation of the presence of the adult's real power. Even as their presence forces
the children to withdraw, breaking off their game, so their grief blights
the innocence of that play. The children have been forced into the position of "Enemies": of the dead, in accordance with the pressure of the
adults' morality; but also of the adults, who have tainted their innocence.
Thus the children are driven away from the literal gravesite, where their
play made death a part of life, and from their innocence in doing so. Looking back "to see how far / It is" is to measure the distance between innocence and acculturation.

An important aspect of the tease in the voice of innocence is the way it
reveals in its very performance how much of a fabrication it is. Even as
the writer of the poem is, after all, an adult taking on the voice of a child,
so the purity of that child's voice in stanzas one and two cannot help but
be undermined by the experience of stanza three. That innocence, we are
told twice over, is nigh impossible to maintain in culture—if it ever ex-
isted. To play at innocence is to imagine, more than it is to remember, to

evoke a condition that is out of culture in order to assess the culture. Yet the changes postulated by such a critique would not be a return to innocence, but a difference that has learned something from enacting it. Consequently, Dickinson's child voice expresses difference rather than absence, as it is situated in rather than apart from culture. Its ingenuousness constitutes a ploy, or a tease, to protect that difference in the process of revealing it.

II

Tease, a matter of voice, is readily apparent in poems where Dickinson adopts personae like the hick or the child. However, her own voice, that of the woman poet, speaks Dickinson's most profound tease. The woman poet, as many have shown, is the outsider writ large—like the bad little girl, she is a contradiction in terms. Neither the normative woman nor the normative poet, she speaks of and to our culture from its margins. This is why, in poems that are not funny at all, Dickinson offers us the possibilities of the essentially comic vision of the tease. Comic because it affirms not only life but the potential for change, in the very teeth of the silence that culture, filling the little girl's mouth with ice, demands from her. "Silence is all we dread. / There's Ransom in a Voice – ," Dickinson writes (1251). Sometimes it is necessary for the voice to tease to speak at all, but it is just that performance that can ransom us, if it can make us complicit in its assertions. The tease requires of us not only that we note its occurrence (because in poems that tease Dickinson foregrounds the poem's existence as language act), but that we participate in whatever meaning we assign to it. In the end, she may have escaped behind her seven veils, but we are left with an altered perspective.[5]

> Good to hide, and hear 'em hunt!
> Better, to be found,
> If one care to, that is,
> The Fox fits the Hound –
>
> Good to know, and not tell,
> Best, to know and tell,
> Can one find the rare Ear,
> Not too dull –   (842)

This poem is an aesthetics of tease: Dickinson's own comments about the ideas which I have been developing. It is in the lacuna between hiding and being found, not telling and telling all, that her poems generally happen. Telling all, being found would be candor rather than the performance of candor, the "only wile." Such openness would be dependent upon the rare ear, the fox fitting the hound. But this is the ideal, the dream, the hope—not the rule, the quotidian.[6] Foxes and readers are too often enemies rather than potential peers. On the other hand, hiding while hearing them hunt, knowing and not telling, while preferable to being found by the wrong hound, is not the condition of poetry. Poetry means speech, not silence—taking risks, coming out of the hiding place: but coming out in costume and makeup, in performance.

Because to hide and hear 'em hunt, to know and not tell, is a tease, meant to entice the hound, or the ear. "I know but I'm not going to tell you" usually translates readily into "see if you can make me tell!" (In her discussion of this poem, Cynthia Griffin Wolff quotes psychologist D. W. Winnicott, who notes of the developing ego: "It is a joy to be hidden but a disaster not to be found" [129].) And so, having induced the fox into the open, the hound comes forward to meet her/him; and this is the place, as I have been suggesting, where the poem happens. A safe space, because if the ear turns out to be, in fact, too dull, it will hear the wile and not the candor. A risky space, because if the fox just happens to fit the hound, a real connection could transpire. Or perhaps it's the other way around. A fit between fox and hound could bring safety, and the risk would come from a hound who didn't understand, who as a consequence might lure the fox forward for the kill. Because tease is the condition for a poetry of risk, we can find it informing many of her poems on the most serious of subjects: on love, death, and, especially, on poetry. When a power relationship is inferred—between beloved and the lover, between death and the living, between speaker and audience—Dickinson will experience both the danger and the attraction of the situation. Into the breach between hiding and being found she will send a teasing speaker, who can in this way incarnate her interest, her anger, her fear. Tease makes it possible for her to challenge these powers, while at the same time it keeps her safe from being punished for doing so. Observing how she teases in some of these poems gives us access to Dickinson's moral vision at its most comic.

In the following poem Dickinson's speaker is caught at just the moment when, in love, she could win by succumbing to the lover's power and thereby receive his protection/affection or win by asserting the power of her own integrity and selfhood (or lose by asserting the power of her integrity, lose by succumbing to his power). Which of these is failing with land in sight, I wonder, reminded of another of her metaphors for the same difficulty as described in poem 405: "It might be easier / To fail – with Land in Sight – / Than – gain – My Blue Peninsula – / To perish – of Delight – ." At such a moment, the tease is absolutely necessary—as both defense and offense, which is what teasing means.

> The Drop, that wrestles in the Sea –
> Forgets her own locality –
> As I – toward Thee –
>
> She knows herself an incense small –
> Yet *small* – she sighs – if *All* – is *All* –
> How *larger* – be?
>
> The Ocean – smiles – at her Conceit –
> But *she*, forgetting Amphitrite –
> Pleads – "Me?"   (284)

This tease is directed both at the person directly addressed by the poem, the "Thee," and the larger reading audience. How you read this poem, and its message, depends on how you hear the voice. Does the final word, "Me?," sound like a challenge, a supplication, a vindication, a caress, a whine? That has to do with how you read the poem that leads up to it, a poem which carefully juxtaposes self-assertion ("wrestles," "locality," "Conceit") against submission ("forgets," "small"). Is the first stanza a compliment: "I forget my sense of self in the larger presence of you"? Or is it a cry of dismay: "I am struggling to maintain my memory of my own 'locality' in the space of your power over me!" How do we interpret the pseudo-syllogism of stanza two: "if *All* – is *All* – / How *larger* – be?" That the drop is equivalent to the sea—one small area of water being the same as the larger area? Or that by subsuming herself in him, she thereby takes on his identity? Is the Ocean's smile pleased or condescending? Does he think she is conceited or clever with words? Does she forget Amphitrite because she herself has now assumed the role of sea-goddess, consort and equal to that of Poseidon, the god of the sea? Or is she foolishly forgetting the fact that he is already married, lord of one submissive wife already? In the face of his smile, she cannot help but plead, "Me?" What does she mean?

My look at the poem highlights its doubleness, but that is not the way a reader usually reads. Usually, we choose one of these voices, and positions, and hear just that. This is a poem about self-assertion! Or, this is a poem about the necessary submission of the female to the male! We believe what we want to believe, what she is letting us believe. Now you see it, now you don't. But as soon as we get a clue of the doubleness, just one sense that there is another way to see it, and to hear it, we suspect how she is teasing us. And Poseidon, to boot. The lover to whom this poem is directly addressed can see also what he wants to see—the sweet little good girl, or the exciting bad girl. She has protected herself, even as she has flaunted her attractiveness, manifested most directly in her skill with words, her "Conceit." The poem is most certainly a come-on, with decidedly sexual overtones. It is as well a cultural critique, its very doubleness both demonstrating and challenging gender-based assumptions about women, men, sexuality, and power. It clearly shows the lure of patriarchal power. But it also gives a voice to the presumptuous female who wants to maintain her own locality, even as it demonstrates by its very form, by its very need to tease, how dangerous a position this is.

Almost all of Dickinson's poems that address the subject of romantic or sexual love can be shown to tease, just as almost all address themselves to issues of identity and power. Poem 211, "Come slowly – Eden!," surely one of the most famous of these, is a good example. It raises the issue of whether the consummation of desire is advisable, and on what terms.

> Come slowly – Eden!
> Lips unused to Thee –
> Bashful – sip thy Jessamines –
> As the fainting Bee –
>
> Reaching late his flower,
> Round her chamber hums –
> Counts his nectars –
> Enters – and is lost in Balms.   (211)

The tease presents itself with the opening line, as "Eden" is importuned to "Come slowly." There is a contradiction, of course, between the "come" and the "slowly" and this is exactly the gesture that I have been describing: a do and don't signal that teases the addressee. For one thing, it requires of the one addressed that he, or she, decide how to proceed.

"Eden" is the one thus addressed. Is "Eden" a person or a situation? Probably both. That is, Eden is subsequently addressed as "Thee," in the following line, a Thee who thereafter possesses Jessamines. What we have is a metaphoric complex, in which a beloved is equated both to a flower and to paradise, so that the feeling and the situation that is love become intertwined and embodied in the lover to whom the poem is addressed.

If figurative language expands the significance of the addressee, turning him or her into love embodied, it contracts the speaker into a single pair of lips. All desire is reduced to the sensation of oral gratification, as these lips find themselves sipping, albeit bashfully, the flowers of the beloved. The result of this image is surely an intensification of the desire that fuels the opening words, "come slowly." But the desire is complicated by the speaker's unfamiliarity and perhaps discomfort with it: "lips unused to Thee." Hence the need for the tease. The addressee is being asked to take the responsibility for what is happening, because the speaker is needy, afraid, bold, bashful—all at once.

A shift in the locus of responsibility, and action, is exactly what transpires, as the poem suddenly switches into an analogy that begins, "As the fainting Bee." Direct address has proved too uncomfortable, too dangerous. What if the thee "came" completely? What if he/she didn't "come"? The directions offered, "Come slowly," admit for both possibilities. Consequently, the action of the poem moves to the story of a bee and a flower—a cautionary tale, surely, for both speaker and addressee. What is literally happening between them is suspended for the duration of the analogy, a kind of coitus interruptus.

"As the fainting Bee – / Reaching late his flower, / Round her chamber hums – / Counts his nectars – / Enters – and is lost in Balms." One major change that transpires in the shift from literal to figurative situation, as commentators on this poem cannot help but notice, is that from passive to active, receptivity to agency. If the bee is now a stand-in for the speaker, the bee is doing the coming, not waiting for the coming to occur. Of course, that transition was actually taking place in the "literal" plane of the rhetoric, as the lips first asked Eden to come slowly, then began a busy albeit bashful sipping, even as Eden (active—coming) turned into a flower, its jessamines being sipped. The very fact of such a transition may be why the shift into analogy seemed necessary, all of a sudden, as the speaker found herself moving from a passive lack of responsibility ("I asked him/her to come slowly") to the act of sipping.

The busy bee of the analogy gets right down to it: circles his flower's chamber, pauses briefly to count his nectars (equivalent to something like counting his blessings or his money—maybe a little of both), and then enters, penetrates the flower, and reaches his goal, or his reward: he is lost in balms. The image is unavoidably sexual, with the bee playing male to the flower's female. The result of desire, the "Eden" of the poem's first line, is to be lost. Lost in balms, in all that fragrance of jessamines, in that lubricous chamber, but definitely lost, not found. Many of Dickinson's poems on this topic deal with the ambivalence of being lost in balms: for example, "The Drop, that wrestles in the Sea," in which the drop forgets her own locality. If we concentrate on this poem, however, there are clues about the profound ambivalence of its closing, all the way from the "come slowly with which the poem begins. Balms are balms and lost is lost: which is it to be, the poem asks but does not answer. The finale, the climax, is after all hypothetical, analogical. The bee in the story may be lost in balms, but the speaker is not: she is left in media res, sipping jessamines. Will she continue on to enter, or to withdraw? The poem, and she, won't say. We, and the poor thee, are left with the tease: the request to come slowly, the forward gesture on behalf of the speaker's lips, in both speaking and sipping, and the cautionary tale these lips tell concerning what becomes of bees who do not stop at sipping. The contemporary term, "cock tease," might well come to mind in this situation, except that part of Emily Dickinson's perplexity, ambivalence, and hence need to tease has to do with how she considers her own role in the enterprise: is she "feminine" or "masculine," and what does this mean in terms of, and to, the beloved to whom the poem is addressed?

We are left, we and the thee, with the poem; with, I would suggest, the powerful sensation of desire which is the poem's one and only surety. It's a very sexy poem, as everyone who reads it has to admit. The poem emits a desire that is not, at least in the poem, at least not literally, appeased. There is no climax: no lessening of desire, but no consequences from it, either. What we experience is pure tease—which is actually pretty exciting.

Love as subject regularly demands tease as performance. Wanting to feel the feeling, wary of its consequences—hundreds of Dickinson's poems are concerned with this problem. Tease is Dickinson's habitual solution: the rhetorical procedure that makes possible the representation of desire—both the speaker's and the beloved's (the reader's). Such poems are comedy rather than tragedy precisely because they have no resolution, no climax. Poised always before the prospect of fulfillment, these poems raise desire to an art in its own right.

Nonetheless, some of Dickinson's poems do examine the issue and consequences of "fulfillment"—or what happens when you don't hold out. If, however, their subject is release or vulnerability, their procedure is anything but. Under these circumstances, tease is needed more than ever. In poem 861, meaning is swathed in veil after veil of ambiguity. The "Sceptic Thomas" to whom the poem is addressed exemplifies the powerful lover, or reader, of whom Dickinson has good reason to be wary.

> Split the Lark – and you'll find the Music –
> Bulb after Bulb, in Silver rolled –
> Scantily dealt to the Summer Morning
> Saved for your Ear when Lutes be old.

Loose the Flood – you shall find it patent –
Gush after Gush, reserved for you –
Scarlet Experiment! Sceptic Thomas!
Now, do you doubt that your Bird was true? (861)

Is this a poem about death or love? Martyrdom or transformation? Poetry or orgasm? And more importantly, why can't we tell? It's a beautiful poem—exciting and lush—and a well-known one, too, with every commentator on it sure that her or his reading surpasses and excludes all the others. I would maintain that in its multiple imagery—its Music, Bulb, Silver, Lute, Flood, Gush, and Scarlet—it teases both subject and audience—if only because that subject is a life and death matter.

"Split the Lark," it begins; this outrageous order is addressed, we discover by the last line of the stanza, to a "you" further identified at the poem's end as a "Sceptic Thomas." If "split" is read as murder, a lark gutted, bisected, what follows is the immolation of an innocent victim, all so that this particular doubting Thomas can see for himself that death, if not resurrection, has occurred. But "split" may be violent without being death-dealing, as the revelation of the "Music" curled within might suggest. Although some have seen those bulbs rolled in silver as something akin to dead fetuses, it is equally likely to see them as being born into the world through this process. If this is a poem about sex, or even about birth, then the splitting would be necessary to release the hidden treasure.

Music comes in bulbs, and bulbs come rolled in silver. Metaphors condense as well as amplify. Music/nascence/riches serve as an overlapping image for the wealth that the birth of art must be. This embryonic music has been hoarded, saved for the "you" to whom the poem is addressed.

Ah, but the sceptic Thomas wants it now. Wants to make sure it's really there. Perhaps the hoarded music is a kind of virginity, literal or figurative. Perhaps the saving was an act of self-defense as much as frugality. We are reminded of other words of Dickinson's: not only "We – would rather / From Our Garret go / White – Unto the White Creator – / Than invest – Our Snow – " (709), but also "Come slowly – Eden!" (211). The former are from a poem about literary publication; the latter from a poem about love. We recall as well: "Good to know, and not tell, / Best, to know and tell, / Can one find the rare Ear / Not too dull – " (842). The not telling has more to do with inadequate listeners than with not wanting to speak. The music in poem 861 has in fact been saved for Thomas' ear: probably because the lark thought it was a rare ear. But what if it wasn't? Better to hoard a treasure than release it indiscriminately. And of course, the longer it has been saved, the harder it is to unlock the coffers—and perhaps, the stronger the yearning to do so. "Come slowly – Eden! / Lips unused to Thee – / Bashful – sip thy Jessamines – ." The subject that the poem seems to be circling is virginity, a condition that has artistic as well as sexual connotations for this poet.

The second stanza may be offering us, and the sceptic Thomas, another example, with "Loose the Flood" paralleling "Split the Lark," or it may be read as a continuation of what happens when the lark is split. The second reading seems more helpful to me, if only because the flood has been "reserved" for him in exactly the same way as the music was saved—for his ear. That is, when the lark is split, the flood is loosed: as the bulbs unroll from their silver wrappings they spill out, flood-like, blood-like. This torrent is patent, the word compressing its several meanings—evident, privileged, protected—into one image that neatly emblemizes the poem's concerns. Such an effusion could be death, orgasm, or birth: it is, in any case, a "Scarlet Experiment."

The experiment has been conducted on behalf of the sceptical Thomas, who, like his namesake, has refused to accept the presence of the "music" on faith. The music, as the final line reveals, instantiates the bird's fidelity. It had indeed been reserved for him, but he needed to see it to believe it. Like the reader of the poem, Thomas's desire requires not only embodiment but understanding. He wants to know what he is getting. However, once seen, released, revealed, it is dead. But why did the addressee's lack of faith result in the murder of his beloved bird? Elsewhere Dickinson has written, "A word is dead / When it is said, / Some say. / I say it just / Begins to live / That day" (1212). Maybe because this reader/lover didn't turn out to be the rare ear, after all. Maybe the suitability of the You has everything to do with whether or not one's words live, or die.

If this is so, we can understand the speaker's unease and even anger—"Now, do you doubt that your Bird was true?"; we can appreciate her fear and lack of confidence—in herself and in the recipient of her music, that ear. It's terrifying to find yourself so vulnerable, so naked. Was it worth it, is the implicit question in the poem's final two lines.

The multiple meanings, or glimpses of them—the overlap of metaphor until it is impossible to tell wherein the literal lies—constitute the tease of such a poem, a tease which seems necessary for the poem to come into language at all. This poem is, in fact, the opposite sort of utterance from the kind that it takes as its subject, that scarlet experiment. Rather than being an unrestrained outpouring of truth, this poem is as guarded as it is gorgeous. It will not take the kind of risk it describes, not even for such a one as the sceptic Thomas might (or might not) be: a rare ear. Because of course what the poem in its ambiguity reveals is that one cannot tell whether the scarlet experiment will end in birth or in death. Better to stay protected, to tease the idea of total and orgasmic release into linguistic existence, but at the same time guard it from the potential repercussions that absolute conviction might provoke. Better to flirt, to lure, to tease— the audience and the subject—when what is at stake is so powerful, so potentially irredeemable. For if Thomas is a suspicious ear—he will not believe, after all—then we, too, are equally suspect. Desired, of course, sought out and sought after—but always dubious, to Dickinson's way of thinking.

III

As "Split the Lark" demonstrates, poetry, love, and death are necessarily related in Dickinson's poetry. Consequently, death as well as love becomes an occasion for the tease. In poems about death, tease reveals again the two different but related functions that I have been describing: first, destabilizing existing definitions; second, flirting—the invitation of desire. Vis-à-vis death, tease is used as a procedure for investigation; the preferred methodology for trying to understand this most evasive, most mysterious— most teasing—of subjects. How do we know what death is, and how do we know to where it leads? Is immortality possible, viable, attainable? Is death the "Hyphen" (poem 1454) between life and immortality, or is it the end of everything? How could we find out? Tease as a procedure for destabilizing definitions is particularly appropriate in this context, for as Dickinson points out over and over, neither the Christian belief in a Heaven for the soul nor science's belief in a dissolution for the body will do it. Ultimately, both represent systems of belief, however culturally sanctified. From her perspective as outside the normative systems of knowledge and belief—neither clergyman nor scientist—she can work at and worry its meaning. Consequently, Dickinson's poems about death scrupulously unravel its meaning from those definitions already in existence.

Tease has another function in some poems that Dickinson writes about death, poems that are directly related to her poems about love. For there is a difference between death as subject or theme and death as presence, a force with which one finds oneself in a personal relationship. In these poems Dickinson's tease operates as it does with a lover: luring death forward, tasting his presence, experiencing it, without committing herself to him. Investigation may be part of her motivation here, but another part is certainly thrill. This is one reason why the connection with erotics seems appropriate. With death, as with love, poetry becomes the opportunity to have the feeling, a dangerous feeling, without taking the consequences or paying the price.

On the other hand, death as lover represents male power in its most extreme form, perhaps because one cannot ever, finally, hold out against him. Death forces the issue of competition which for Dickinson is just beneath the surface of erotic interchange. With him, it's a life and death struggle, literally, so that her tease is on behalf of self-preservation. At the same time, however, Dickinson yearns toward him precisely because he does possess this ultimate power, because she cannot control him with her charm, her skill, her words. Thus she reveals something about her own acculturation. Even rebels belong to that which they rebel against, and this is shown most dramatically in the war of tease between Dickinson's speakers and death.

There are many poems in which Dickinson teases cultural definitions of death, and some are even funny.

> We pray – to Heaven –
> We prate – of Heaven –
> Relate – when Neighbors die –
> At what o'clock to Heaven – they fled –
> Who saw them – Wherefore fly?
>
> Is Heaven a Place – a Sky – a Tree?
> Location's narrow way is for Ourselves –
> Unto the Dead
> There's no Geography –
>
> But State – Endowal – Focus –
> Where – Omnipresence – fly?   (489)

In Dickinson's examination of the nature of death and immortality, the Christian concept of Heaven frequently takes a large brunt of her critique. In this little poem, she mocks the literalness of the doctrine and, especially, of the belief of her community. "Is Heaven a Place – a Sky – a Tree," she laughs, even as she demands of her praying and prating neighbors: who actually saw dead people go to this place we call Heaven? why would someone need to fly to get there?

Against this literalization she offers disembodied abstraction: state, endowal, focus—omnipresence. The point about these abstractions is exactly that one cannot image them. Therefore, neither will the poem. To call attention to this one fact that is known, the poem concludes by deconstructing an image in mid-flight. "Where – Omnipresence – fly?" Against our impulse to put wings on the dead and see them soaring off to Heaven, she poses the word Omnipresence. You can't do it, she demonstrates, and you can't imagine it: wings, a white gown, a little gold halo on an omnipresence.

This poem begins to tease the meaning of death by setting aside the obvious, clearly simplistic and fallacious definitions to make a space for something else. Here the something else is deliberately non-literal, non-imagistic. It escapes representation even as it is represented. All the poems that tease death and its ramifications suggest in one way or another that what they are circling is a mystery, and that is what language needs to tease out. Other such poems pursue the endeavor.

> Of Paradise' existence
> All we know
> Is the uncertain certainty –
> But it's vicinity infer,
> By it's Bisecting
> Messenger –   (1411)

"Uncertain certainty." This explanation is so important because it is not its opposite—certain uncertainty. That is, even though the existence of Paradise is always uncertain, never proved or provable, that very uncertainty is a sure thing. It is something, not nothing. The oxymoron, "uncertain certainty," sets up exactly the same tension that is inherent in all the words denoting death and a possible life after it: the strain between the necessity for representation (something is there) and the difficulty in achieving it (what is there you cannot see, cannot know). This poem goes on to point to inferring as the mode of knowing, and hence, the way toward representation. To infer is to go from what evidence there is to what evidence there is not. As a methodology, it sits somewhere between guessing and reasoning; it is like teasing. In the case of this poem, the evidence one has is the Bisecting Messenger, which I take to be death. Death is a certainty which points us toward the uncertainty, the "vicinity" of Paradise. In this poem, the evidence, death, gets a concrete if metaphoric image, Bisecting Messenger, while Paradise gets an oxymoronic abstraction, uncertain certainty. Both the metaphor and the oxymoron are linguistic ways of teasing out a truth that is always hidden.

Although linguistic abstraction seems one way in which to write death's mystery, it is troublesome as a poetic strategy. For one thing, it is hard to do, because language keeps resisting this pull away from its representational function. Perhaps even more important, however, is the fact that abstraction intensifies rather than mitigates the fear that death evokes precisely because it is a gap at the center of everything.[7] An early poem sets out this very problem for us.

Dust is the only Secret –
Death, the only One
You cannot find out all about
In his "native town."

Nobody knew "his Father" –
Never was a Boy –
Had'nt any playmates,
Or "Early history" –

Industrious! Laconic!
Punctual! Sedate!
Bold as a Brigand!
Stiller than a Fleet!

Builds, like a Bird, too!
Christ robs the Nest –
Robin after Robin
Smuggled to Rest!   (153)

The personification in this poem is clearly a ploy, a linguistic gesture flung out in the face of its acknowledged fallacy. Death had no native town, had no father. However, the very act of giving shape to this lack makes it possible to imagine the shape, so that the rest of the poem proceeds to use its fiction of embodiment to offer the possibility of salvation. Once the fiction of bird and nest is created, then the idea of another bird, Christ, who could rob the nest, can be reified. In this fashion personification becomes the linguistic means to tease out death's existence, to confront its power. Without this essentially human gesture, as Dickinson shows us in another of her many poems about dying, death's mystery becomes too overwhelming. If poem 153 is lightheartedly certain about Christ's power to intervene on behalf of Heaven, poem 286 hypothesizes what would happen if He could not. Here, too, imagery is at work to give some sort of understandable shape to what Dickinson elsewhere calls the "White Exploit" (922), but the underlying purpose of these shapes is, paradoxically, to reveal once again death's terrible abstraction.

That after Horror – that 'twas *us* –
That passed the moldering Pier –
Just as the Granite Crumb let go –
Our Savior, by a Hair –

A second more, had dropped too deep
For Fisherman to plumb –
The very profile of the Thought
Puts Recollection numb –

The possibility – to pass
Without a Moment's Bell –
Into Conjecture's presence –
Is like a Face of Steel –
That suddenly looks into our's
With a metallic grin –
The Cordiality of Death –
Who drills his Welcome in –   (286)

Stanza three presents the "possibility": the idea of arriving at death without the intervention of the Fisherman, Christ, who, in the first two stanzas, is shown to have saved the drowning, dying humans "by a Hair." But the poem's emphasis is on the what if, even though it continues to protect us all, readers and subjects alike, by insisting on the hypothetical nature of a "Thought" that "Puts recollection numb – ." In the final stanza, death is first represented as "Conjecture's presence," a phrase which seems important enough to pause over. Yet another oxymoron, reminiscent of the "uncertain certainty," it likewise juxtaposes known against unknown, here against where. Conjecture, like the word "infer," stands once again for the mystery and riddle that defies reasoned investigation. The presence of conjecture is therefore not so much a negation as a living horror, like conjuring up a ghost during a seance. The phrase is just too dreadful to be allowed to last; it is followed quickly by an image, a representation that, in its personification, is not as frightening as the abstract words which preceded it. We see the "Face of Steel" with its "metallic grin," a smile like a lethal weapon (it is). The impact of "drills" (or "nails," in an alternate version) against "Welcome" is altogether terrible. But as an idea one can live with it more easily than the thought of Conjecture's presence.

Consequently, death personified becomes important and necessary to
Dickinson. In such poems, we see the two big teasers, Death and Dickinson, performing together. Unfortunately, representing death in human
form leads irrevocably to the understanding that his tease is stronger, a
force against which there is no protection.

> Death is the supple Suitor
> That wins at last –
> It is a stealthy Wooing
> Conducted first
> By pallid innuendoes
> And dim approach
> But brave at last with Bugles
> And a bisected Coach
> It bears away in triumph
> To Troth unknown
> And Kinsmen as divulgeless
> As throngs of Down –   (1445)

This is a companion poem to the better-known 712, "Because I could
not stop for Death – ," with its image of death as the courtly lover in his
carriage. Here, however, the emphasis is more clearly on the lover and his
character, and here we see how tease structures his "supple" activities.
His "stealthy Wooing," "pallid innuendoes," and "dim approach" are just
that much more frightening because they toy with the subject, rather than
offering a frontal attack, just finishing her off! Attack? But this is a lover!
Yes. A lover who kills, a lover whose ubiquitous power is ultimately revealed as he carries off his victim/bride to the grave.

Why, then, lover? Because there is something both erotic and romantic
about this relationship. Death is alluring as well as luring, courtly in the
attention he pays, sexy in his power and importance. He raises your desire,
that is the interesting thing: you come toward him rather than running
away. Death is, to Dickinson, the ultimate male. Can her tease match
his—her power with words challenge his power with lives?

An important poem that specifically addresses the power of his tease is
315, "He fumbles at your Soul." We are back again to the poems, central
in Dickinson's oeuvre, that are about, all at once, love, death, and poetry.
These experiences "coeval come," because they are the triumvirate at the
heart of the mystery of human existence.

He fumbles at your Soul
As Players at the Keys
Before they drop full Music on –
He stuns you by degrees –
Prepares your brittle Nature
For the Ethereal Blow
By fainter Hammers – further heard –
Then nearer – Then so slow
Your Breath has time to straighten –
Your Brain – to bubble Cool –
Deals – One – imperial – Thunderbolt –
That scalps your naked Soul –

When Winds take Forests in their Paws –
The Universe – is still –   (315)

Pages have been devoted to the identity of the "He" in this poem. Is
He lover? Muse? God? Death? It's hard to tell, because the experience
described, what the "He" does to the "you," could be sex, creativity, salvation, or dying. An all-powerful force descends upon a subject, whose
experience of and with this force appears both terrifying and transcendent.
Images of music, storm, assault, and sexuality converge to suggest the various and related identities for the event in question and for its participants.
As Robert Weisbuch writes, "it is difficult to decide whether the active
force's preparatory visits are benevolent foreshadowings of a final transcendent anguish or extended tortures progressing to a crucial climax. Images of creation and destruction alternate, and the final term of the coda
is silence" (99). What I want to emphasize here is how the behavior of the
aggressor is reminiscent of other figures more clearly identified as Death,
especially in the teasing nature of his come-on. The death figure is frequently conflated with lover and with God, all instances of patriarchal
power, so it should come as no surprise that the same thing happens here,
in this more ambiguous poem. All of these experiences go together, in
Dickinson's mind: they are part of the same gestalt.

In this poem, the stunning by degrees, the aggressor's preferred behavior, has decided elements of the tease. The hammers fainter heard, then
nearer, then so slow remind us of the "stealthy Wooing," the "dim approach" of the supple suitor, Death, in poem 1445, with the same erotic
as well as violent overtones. That this is fascinating as well as horrifying is
made clear not only in the fact that the subject confronts her visitor

calmly, her breath straightened and her brain bubbling cool, but by the image that thereupon follows—thrilling, transcendent, and murderous all at once: "Deals – One – imperial – Thunderbolt – / That scalps your naked soul – " (or "peels" it, in an alternate version). Clearly, this is a death, but it is glorious, it is elevating, taking one to heights never before scaled. It is orgasmic—a figure for whatever else is taking place. As Cristanne Miller writes, "the climax is as ecstatic as it is devastating; the tension of the poem resides in its perfect commingling of the sensations of breathless anticipation and terror" (*A Poet's Grammar* 116). Afterward, there is a kind of holy stillness. In the final couplet the main actors seem to be gone from the poem, replaced by winds and forests, which are either analogous to or metaphoric for the experience that has just taken place. Whatever, whichever the case—either or both—the result is stillness. A curious peace, the aftermath and result of what has just occurred.

Death's tease is not so much a game or a dance as it is a competition. (Maybe that is the difference between male and female tease.) And who wins, after all? Death, you will say. No one can escape him. Yes, but the poetic teasing of death, in all of the modes that I have tried to describe, has its own way, if not of winning, for that is not really its purpose, then of knowing. The words of tease, as they bring the mystery forward, into representation—into analogy, metaphor, image, and personification—leave behind a record, a track or tracking. In the face of steel, into Conjecture's presence, they offer exactly what Dickinson always fears will be lost at death if Christ does not save us into immortality: the power to "know and tell." "Once to achieve, annuls the power / Once to communicate – " (922), she notes about death. Yet these poems speak against the void, the silence, as Dickinson explains in lines which have proved central to this essay:

> Silence is all we dread.
> There's Ransom in a Voice –
> But Silence is Infinity.
> Himself have not a face.   (1251)

Giving him a face, as we have seen, is indeed one way to ransom the captured bride. The poetry of tease offers expression in the teeth of danger. The danger is real, but so are the words.

IV

Focusing on Dickinson's tease in its various manifestations helps us to see in one more way how her poetry is always about language. Language is what occupies the space between offer and refusal, between hiding and being found. There is so much danger, danger that can be identified as generic male power and desired as such; there is so much need to confront it, affront it, win it, use it, change it. All of this is what poetry can do, especially poetry as tease.

Poems that address the subject of poetry are consequently poems that are about tease; that is, they call attention to their own performance. These poems, special if only because they are so rare in Dickinson's canon, are usually about "poets – they"; or "the poet – he." The first and most obvious tease is the fact that, in poems written by her, she does not admit to being a poet. Not outright, not literally—but of course, she does so frequently in "slant" ways—through figure, through allusion, through the games she plays. If in these instances we can show ourselves to rank among those rare ears, figuring out that when she says she would not be a poet, she also postulates being the one who would stun herself with her art, then her achievement, and her secret, is safe with us. If not, if we didn't get it, then she is also safe—from us. Poetry itself is the locus for danger and desire; the truth that must, she has told us, be told slant to be told at all.

> I cannot dance upon my Toes –
> No Man instructed me –
> But oftentimes, among my mind,
> A Glee possesseth me,
>
> That had I Ballet knowledge –
> Would put itself abroad
> In Pirouette to blanch a Troupe –
> Or lay a Prima, mad,
>
> And though I had no Gown of Gauze –
> No Ringlet, to my Hair,
> Nor hopped to Audiences – like Birds,
> One Claw upon the Air,
>
> Nor tossed my shape in Eider Balls,
> Nor rolled on wheels of snow

Till I was out of sight, in sound,
The House encore me so –

Nor any know I know the Art
I mention – easy – Here –
Nor any Placard boast me –
It's full as Opera –   (326)

This poem about performance demands that we notice its performance—which is explicitly that of tease. The poem asks us to think about
how we read it, because it is offering us the chance to be distinguished
from the "any" of ordinary audiences. In this way it becomes a gloss on
"Good to hide, and hear 'em hunt!"

Why do I call this a poem about poetry, when it never mentions the
word? That is the first tease. Dance, Glee, Opera—these are the words
for art and its performance. But even as opera is "full"—of kinds of theater as well as passion, meaning, and beauty—full of song, dance, drama,
and spectacle; even as "glee" means song as well as happiness, so these
words and this vision become a code, an analogy for what this particular
speaker does do—which is, we know from reading the poem, write poetry.
This is our first test as readers: can we tell that this is a poem about poetry?

Tease number two is the poem's negation. Maybe this is a poem about
poetry, but its speaker asserts emphatically in the first line that dancing/
writing is just what she cannot do. Yes and no. For if we follow the poem's
structure and logic more carefully, we see that the negative affirmation of
the opening line is matched by the positive affirmation of the final
line—"It's full as Opera – ," and that the progression from one to the
other occurs by way of the subjunctive. This subjunctive, "had I Ballet
knowledge – ," is used to negotiate the interface between mind and world
that is the thematic focus of the poem as well as its organizing structural
dynamic. First, the negation, "I cannot dance," is immediately juxtaposed
against a positive, "oftentimes, among my mind, / A Glee possesseth me."
The Glee is there, in her mind. "That had I Ballet knowledge – / Would
put itself abroad." The issue has to do with inner and outer, with inner
presence and external expression. Ballet knowledge would enable her to
perform what is there inside, to bring it from private to public, from protected to exposed, from desire to fulfillment.

But she doesn't have it—right? Yet if this is true, how does she manage
to perform the next three stanzas, which are a detailed, and funny, rendition of a ballet production? As the speaker proceeds to represent the dan-

cers with their gowns of gauze, the ringlets in their hair, hopping away as birds do, "One Claw upon the Air," spinning in their tutus like "Eider Balls," rolling "on wheels of snow," we see both their performance and hers. And yet through it all the speaker continues to insist, via negation, that she has no gown of gauze, she has not hopped to audiences. Suddenly, if we read carefully, these negatives take on yet more meaning. There is not only the distinction between what she can do in her mind and what she can do out there, but between what she can do with her body and with words. This turns out to be a poem about poetry, not about ballet, because the ballet performance takes place here in words, not *en pointe*. It's a glorious performance, precisely because it does foreground its linguistic status. It does so via simile and metaphor. What makes it grand are the images and the humor it creates this way: the birds with their raised claws, the eider balls, the wheels of snow. These are feats of language, not of extension and balance. Dancing is an analogy for writing, but of course it isn't literal. Dickinson can't dance, but watching her write about dancing helps us to see that she can indeed write.

But what about that ballet knowledge? Does she or doesn't she have it? Yes and no. She has knowledge about it, if not knowledge to do it. Knowledge about informs her literary presentation, but still, as the performance draws to a close, as the ballerinas leave the stage, out of sight, and the audience encores her so with its loud clapping, negation asserts itself: "Nor any know I know the Art / I mention – easy – Here – ." The applauding audience and the ballet performance are all a fantasy, existing in her imagination, recorded in the subjunctive. The association with her poetry, as well as her ballet skills, is readily made. That performance, the fantasy of dancing, the skill of writing it, is not known to audiences: the poems are not being published. Is anybody reading it now? No placard boasts her—neither in front of a theatre—"One night only, Emily Dickinson!"—nor on the cover of a book. Nevertheless, "It's full as Opera – ." "Full" is one of those words, like "ample," that regularly inform Dickinson's writing about her mind, her mental life. "On a Columnar Self – / How ample to rely," she writes in a poem that concludes, "Suffice Us – for a Crowd – " (789). "It's full"—the mind, the inner life. Full as Opera. The Glee that oftentimes possesseth her is indeed a happiness as well as a song. The inner life cannot be discounted as not being there, not being real. Nonetheless, an audience, oh, an audience, the sound of the applause, the call for an encore, wouldn't that be grand? Or, would it? What would they see? What would they understand? Would they applaud—or jeer?

If you manage to read this poem past its superficial denials, seeing through or past the veils as they spin around you, you are a possible audience, a potential lover. If so, the tease itself has delighted you, lured you, raised your own desire to see inside. To see it: that which is full as Opera. But of course, you didn't, not really. You saw what was there—the words, the poem—never it.

The poet as tease: this is the voice of the bad girl, who will not be silenced, who will come out in words before the world. Simply by speaking, this poet puts into question all laws and rules. Consequently, the world of the poem, that space between inside and outside, safety and danger, becomes an alternative world, standing in critical relation to its readers and the culture in which they reside and read. Sometimes Dickinson is lighthearted about its worth and its reality. This is her egalitarian vision of the disruption of hegemony and hierarchy: there is a place for them and for me.

> I send Two Sunsets –
> Day and I – in competition ran –
> I finished Two – and several Stars –
> While He – was making One –
>
> His own was ampler – but as I
> Was saying to a friend –
> Mine – is the more convenient
> To Carry in the Hand –   (308)

Here Dickinson abolishes the idea of competition itself, the necessity for power, that informs all of her discourse on love, on death, on male-female (read world-poem) relationships. "Day" stands for nature, maybe God, because creativity and creation are at issue in this little poem. The competition between Day and the speaker sees them hurriedly at work, after the starting gun goes off. She manages to finish two sunsets, as well as several stars, while he makes only one.

But in the second stanza, a change in attitude occurs. Competition is undermined when the speaker acknowledges that the criteria for winning and losing are variable. Quantity is one, but so is size; and so is function. His is bigger, hers is more convenient. So who won? Neither, or both. Winning is no longer the issue. There is room, and need, for both. Of course, these "sunsets" exist in different worlds: that of nature and that of language. Her poem about sunset can be carried in the hand; nature's sunsets are out there to color the world. Poetry and nature are therefore not in competition with one another, at least according to this poem, which effectively discounts the very need for tease with its assertions. This is indeed a comic conclusion, with everybody living happily ever after.[8]

However, most of the time, this fortuitous world-view is not possible. Dickinson's comedy is not a matter of the underdog winning and taking over the world. Rather, it affirms life by creating a breathing space, the poem, where alternatives to the cultural norms can abide. No matter that, as I have been discussing, this kind of living is chancy and fraught; it is there. I began this investigation of the poet as tease with a poem in which the little girl who tried to tease is silenced; her words cut short by the coldness, the ice that fills her mouth. In this poem it is difficult to distinguish between a good girl and a dead girl: there is no substantive difference between saying please and saying nothing. A living girl, however, is a bad girl: bad because, we can expostulate, she teases. No matter how problematic teasing has been shown to be, in all of its manifestations and variations, it is an exploit in the face of silence, of silencing. Consequently, the "death" that is frequently associated with it, with poetry, as well as with its concomitant expression, love, cannot be the same death as the one that turns a teasing girl into a corpse. One death brings nothing, and that is tragedy; the other death brings transformation, and that is comedy, as the following poem reveals.

> To pile like Thunder to its close
> Then crumble grand away
> While Everything created hid
> This – would be Poetry –
>
> Or Love – the two coeval come –
> We both and neither prove –
> Experience either and consume –
> For None see God and live –   (1247)

This poem has been dogging my words throughout this essay. Why, we might ask, when in its evocation of the grandeur of a violent storm, which proves to be analogous to the experience of poetry, or love, or God, an experience which ends, in the final lines, in death, the poem seems more like Wagnerian tragedy than comedy. However, upon closer look, we see that it, too, is a tease. Not only does it tease accepted definitions, replacing them with an outlandish and apocalyptic definition of its own, but it shrouds that definition in mystery, the veils of tease, created by its own language, so that once again we as readers are seduced into both wanting and trying to understand that meaning. And because this particular mystery—

of the relationship between poetry, love, and death—stands at the very center of Dickinson's personal and aesthetic desire, the urgency to tell it and the necessity of protecting it combine to give this poem the charged intensity that has made it one of Dickinson's most important lyrics. For finally, what is seen and not seen is the power and import of expression without the slant, or tease—an ideal of poetry or love that comes to us pure, total, without disguise.

The opening image of the thunderstorm provides atmosphere, environment. And yet there is more here than that storm; for, while the storm words focus us appropriately on sound, on voice (the gradual intensifying and lessening of the thunder), other words, "pile" and "crumble," are not only visual in import but instrumental in creating a different metaphor: of a wall, an edifice. To make a sound which ceases, to build a structure that decomposes, "This – would be Poetry – ." But there is actually more to the double analogy. There is the "grand" in "crumble grand away," so that we really cannot read the second part of the cycle as loss or even deprivation, not when the cessation is "grand." There is also the reaction of the audience: "While Everything created hid." The event is monumental, terrific, awesome enough so that the world (the audience, the reader) tries to hide from it, rather as we do before an eclipse. One cannot encounter it with naked vision. This, then, is like poetry: an event of monumental proportions, apocalyptic and grand, in both its rise and its ebb.

Like events in nature, but not: an analogy. Analogy twice over, for poetry and, begins the second stanza, for love: "the two coeval come." Coeval: of the same age, date, or duration. Not the same thing, not equivalent, but occurring together—contemporaries. Lock and key, horse and carriage—love and poetry (not love and marriage). Which means, I think, that as the song says, "you can't have one without the other."

The second stanza, now devoted to the experience of the reader, even as the first stanza focused on the act of composition, on the writer, demonstrates this "togetherness": "We both and neither prove – "; "Experience either and consume – ." Both and neither, either link poetry and love as functioning in the same way, or at the same time. These lines are particularly difficult to interpret (they are such a tease), because they document the heart of the mystery. There is mystery in proving and not proving, all at once. There is also mystery in consuming/being consumed—for it is difficult to tell which form of the verb is meant.[9]

What we see is a simultaneous active/passive, positive/negative. Our experience of poetry/love at this level is different from everyday reality; it has taken us to another plane of existence altogether. Such experience is like, is equated with, seeing God and with the death this brings about. "For

None see God and live – " recalls the imperial thunderbolt of poem 315 that scalps your naked soul, even as it circles back to the first analogy in this poem, of the thunderstorm, during which everything created hid. This hiding, averting the naked eyes, is thus related to the not living of the final lines, a death which is clearly not literal. If one were to see God after death, one would be in Heaven, no longer "dead." If one sees God during life, the death thus experienced is a transformation, not an extinction. An ultimate, transcendent, spiritual event. Like poetry or love. One cannot prove it by scientific or mathematical means, but one can experience (prove) it, and even show in the process that one has the character or ability necessary to experience it properly. If we are consumed by it, we also consume: we are changed, even reborn. According to Joanne Feit Diehl, "such a moment of annunciation breaks through mortality to create an altered condition which marks an irrevocable change" (79). Resonances of the eucharist enhance this image, connoting a Christ who has intervened between us and both death and God the father. If the storm piles up and then crumbles down, it will pile up again. Transformation is the opposite of perishing, so that in this poem literal death is thwarted by poetry and love.

This poem is a tease in its linguistic density, its expression and protection of its meaning, but it is also an explanation of the tease that I have been documenting throughout Dickinson's poetry. For it points to a poetry, and a love, without tease. It describes what happens when the reader has the rare ear, the strength as well as the desire, to experience poetry that is unmitigated. The result is the exact opposite of what happens in "Split the Lark," or in "They won't frown always." The sceptic Thomas with his lark, the adults with their little girl read as representatives of their culture, and in the process can kill the woman poet. It is from them that she must protect her poem, and herself, by means of her tease. But always there is the belief in the real thing: the right reader, the true poem. The right lover, the true love. A place where we might meet not only as equals but as acolytes, ready to experience the transcending results of our union.

In the meantime, as the little beggar girl of poem 373 put it, Dickinson "decks." She puts on makeup and costume, those gauzy draperies of mystery and language, and teases. As we are drawn into her aura, into her poem with its shakes and its shimmies, as we reach out to hold her and get—ourselves as well as her echo—we understand our own acculturation, the need for her seven veils. As much as we know we want her, we also have to understand our danger to her. However, in the space of her poem both reader and poet get the chance to venture at being rare poet, rare ear. For in and by means of the poem transformation becomes possible, with its altered shapes and arrangements. The poem is just that much outside of culture that this is conceivable. It is just that much inside of culture that this is frightening. Tease is, after all, revelation as well as deferral, invitation as well as inhibition. Dickinson's tease is her agency toward power, because it is what she needs to do to establish the place that is the poem. Here both reader and poet might be ransomed from complete acculturation, coming together to make her (our) new meanings. Thankfully, Dickinson, that bad girl poet, never did forget to tease.

Chapter 3
The Poet as Cartoonist

by Martha Nell Smith

*Miss Emily was apt with a pencil and in a tiny sketch of Amherst,
sent my mother, everything was covered with snow except the
parsonage. With it came a line saying: "I omitted the snow on the
roof, distrusting the premonition, 'Emily.'"*

—MACGREGOR JENKINS,
FRIEND AND NEIGHBOR[1]

*I can best express my contrition in the words of the Prayer of a
Clergyman I heard when a Child – "Oh thou who sittest upon the
Apex of the Cherubim, look down upon this, thine unworthy
Terrapin"!*

—EMILY DICKINSON TO ELIZABETH HOLLAND
(L 806, MARCH 1883)

What Counts as a Cartoon?

Cartoon. [as a noun:] 1. A drawing on stout paper, made as a design
for a painting of the same size to be executed in fresco or oil, or for a
work in tapestry, mosaic, stained glass, or the like. 2. A full-page illustration in a paper or periodical; *esp.* applied to those in the comic papers relating to current events.   (*Oxford English Dictionary*, 1981 ed.)

Cartoon. [as a verb:] 1. To design, as a cartoon (sense 1); to make a
preparatory sketch or tracing of. 2. To represent by a cartoon (sense 2);
to caricature, or hold up to ridicule.   (*O.E.D.*)

Cartoon. 1: a preparatory design, drawing, or painting (as for a
fresco) 2 a: a satirical drawing commenting on public and usu. political
matters b: COMIC STRIP 3: ANIMATED CARTOON—**cartoon** [verb]—
cartoonist [noun]   (*Webster's New Collegiate Dictionary*, 1979 ed.)

ORIGINALLY, "CARTOON" REFERRED TO preliminary drafts to outline designs of artistic works. Now the term has evolved so that most think immediately of the funny papers or the editorial page and seem unaware of the earlier significations of the word "cartoon." Yet connotations of the preparatory pertain to much of the contemporary currency of the word, for a few minutes with the comics often preface one's day, and singular or serial comic illustrations often vent feelings necessary to acknowledge if situations or relationships are to be confronted or shrugged off. Political cartoons like those by Herblock and Ben Sargent[2] frequently lampoon a president or other government official in whom constituents are disappointed; and long-running comic strips like *Blondie* portray tensions of family—the wife spending too much of Dagwood's money or being too preoccupied with her new catering business to fix him dinner—and of the working man—Mr. Dithers exasperated with Bumstead's lackluster performance yet again—to give the audience a chuckle before they must go about the day's business. Cartoons tend to be synecdochical and often represent characters by one distinguishing trait—Pigpen by a cloud of dust, for example—and settings are similarly pared down so that one item or figure stands for a group or institution—*Doonesbury*'s Mike for the Baby Boomers. Implicitly mocking the very notion of realistic artistic/literary representation at the same time that they presume to comment on reality, cartoons translate experience, events, and personalities into portrayals that range from the palatably lighthearted to the unbelievably ludicrous. For example, to make a political point, often through silly exaggeration, cartoons move the field for expression from anything remotely resembling the civility and decorum expected of real negotiation to a field where players can indulge their wildest fantasies in voicing demands and/or characterizing an opponent or issue. Since they present a whimsical world in which anything can happen and from which audiences expect the outrageous, cartoons offer a forum in which the unsayable or unthinkable can be voiced with impunity; they are a way we have, then, of "driving off the spleen" and restraining ourselves from "knocking people's hats off."[3]

Of course, like *Blondie*, cartoons such as *Peanuts, Garfield, Family Circus*, and *Calvin & Hobbes* are usually not voicing the politically irreverent or otherwise unacceptable so much as they are making light of the quotidian frustrations every reader knows all too well: the inability to perform to the home team's advantage on the schoolyard or neighborhood baseball diamond; the cat that demands to be fed when sleepy humans want to relish the deep winks of the wee hours just before dawn; or the bored child who, at his mother's bidding to use his imagination for self-entertainment, concocts a scheme that entails throwing a bucket of cool water on Mom herself, which of course results in his punishment. The comic relief cartoons offer, then, extends from the mildly entertaining smirk at habitual shortcomings like a lack of coordination to the outbursts afforded by the hilarity of a child's or pet's pranks as well as to the guffaw evoked by political judgments rendered when, for example, George Bush's evil twin Skippy in *Doonesbury* is blamed for insincere campaign pledges.[4] The possibility that Emily Dickinson's humor might extend beyond occasional ironic wit to more radical strategies resembling those commonly associated with cartooning has not been seriously entertained. Likewise, the fact that her range of subjects humorously portrayed in previously unstudied sketches and layouts parallel those treated in cartoons—from poking fun at familial tensions to deflating national literary and political figures—has not been widely acknowledged. Especially since a commonplace in biography and literary study has been that she was apolitical and chose to ignore national events, Dickinson's political humor has almost without exception gone unremarked.[5]

Single frame lampoons and comic strips, not the cartoons of television or film, have been rendered above to situate the present-day reader because those cartoons commonly encountered in the print media most nearly resemble Emily Dickinson's handcrafted layouts, sketches, "cartooning" epistolary descriptions, and lyric narratives. The most elucidating analogies between Dickinson's individual layouts and sketches and popular culture works can be drawn to the one-shot spins by her contemporaries featured in humorous periodicals like *Harper's New Monthly Magazine* or *Frank Leslie's Illustrated Newspaper* or to those by our contemporaries—T. O. Sylvester, Gary Larson, Herblock, or Sargent—featured in any metropolitan newspaper.[6] Since the comic strip, with its progressive series of panels, did not assume its present form until the fin de siècle, Dickinson would have been most familiar with illustrations widely recognized as key sources for the genre's origins like those of current events marketed by Leslie, those in children's books such as *The Poetic Gift: or Alphabet in Rhyme* (the household copy has been annotated by Dickinson herself; see Leyda 1:99), or those in novels sketched by George Cruikshank and "Phiz."[7]

Though to call her sketches and layouts "cartoons" makes liberal use of the term, such liberties have been taken since the advent of Dickinson study: to print and distribute the Amherst poet's private "publications" is to make liberal use of the term "literature," which we conventionally associate with the productions of writers who, like Dickinson's contemporaries Hawthorne, Whitman, and Stowe, work specifically to see their writings mechanically reproduced and distributed to as wide an audience as possible. Dickinson's private "publication" of her poems—in letters to friends, acquaintances, famous editors like Thomas Wentworth Higginson, and well-known women writers like Helen Hunt Jackson, and to posterity in the manuscript books found in her room—demands shifts in thinking about what can count for public literature.[8] Similarly, Dickinson's hand-made mode of production shifts the site of the cartoon from the humorous periodical or newspaper to her private communications or records. As it did for her poetry, our study moves her comic text into the public sphere and demands shifts in thinking about what can count as a cartoon. Just as the analogies drawn between Dickinson's privatized literary project and conventional ones that are more public have proved to be an ever-fertile field for literary criticism, so analogies drawn between her private cartooning acts and those more public and familiar serve to open new fields of inquiry for understanding the author and the significance of her cultural work. Entertaining the possibility that her comic drawings and layouts might best be counted as cartoons diversifies understandings both of the scope of her holographic textual production and some limitations that have been imposed when translating those documents for conventional print publication.

    That features of the comic strip as readers now know it did not evolve until developments like those by Richard Outcault of *The Yellow Kid* at the end of the nineteenth century does not mean that Dickinson was unaware of pictorial narratives and did not cartoon in ways that are comparable to the illustrated narratives of the strip. In the final section of this chapter, examining two of Dickinson's highly pictorial lyrics and scrutinizing some animated passages in letters reveal that her texts sometimes function in ways strikingly akin to a Cole or Hogarth series or to the brief narratives of comic strips. Flamboyantly illustrative, moving from exaggerated scene to scene, these depictions caricature events and institutions using strategies similar to those commonly employed in cartoon strips. For example, one of her best-known and most frequently anthologized poems, "I heard a Fly buzz – when / I died – " (F 26; P 465),[9] consists of four stanzas, each of which might be compared to the panels of a four-frame comic strip: in the first stanza appear the deceased and the buzzing fly of which she or he is conscious in the "Stillness" "Between the Heaves of Storm"; in the second appear the mourners with "Eyes . . . wrung . . . dry" waiting for death's big moment; in the third the nearly deceased is willing away her or his earthly "Keepsakes"; and in the fourth, the speaker's eyelids descend in death, accompanied by the fly's "Blue – uncertain stumbling Buzz – ." Though it is not divided into discrete stanzas, "There came a Wind like a

Bugle – " (P 1593) offers similar four-part serial movement: the wind quivering in the grass; humans shutting their windows and doors against the "Emerald Ghost"; the "electric Moccasin" passing over "a strange Mob of panting Trees"; and "the Bell" blowing about "within the steeple wild." Even single sentences like "You remember my ideal cat has always a huge rat in its mouth, just going out of sight" (L 471, August 1876) works serially, suggesting at least a couple of pictures: the cat with its rodent-stuffed mouth; then perhaps just its tail disappearing around a corner.

Still, considering this chapter's title, some readers may wonder, "Doesn't she mean the poet as *cartooned?*" After all, popular American culture—from *Jeopardy* to *Cheers* to *thirtysomething* to Charles Schultz and his *Peanuts* cartoon strip—has gotten much mileage out of snickering about Emily Dickinson. Even Berke Breathed, *Bloom County*'s creator, decided to have a little fun in national election year 1988 when he, following the lead of George Bush, declared that Dickinson's December 10th birthday, like Pearl Harbor Day, is now in—remember?—September. A century of edition after edition of her poems and letters, numerous biographies, a one-woman-show-of-a-play performed around the country and broadcast on PBS, a minute-long biographical sketch produced for CBS, a dance by Martha Graham based on her spirit, a place setting at *The Dinner Party* by Judy Chicago, at least two records of readings, numerous musical settings of her poems, a murder mystery, a ceremonial burial in "The Poet's Corner" at St. John's Cathedral in New York City, and Emily Dickinson raisin brandycakes, cookbooks, and throw pillows for sale all attest to the fact that she is a consumer item in American culture. That one can easily find greeting cards with the effusive excesses of a very young woman just beginning to think of herself as a poet hints at what the two-record set, *Emily Dickinson—A Self-Portrait*, makes clear: it is the idea of Emily in bridal white, pining, made especially sensitive by unrequited love, rather than the prolific poet who wrote Thomas Higginson's wife, "I wish you were strong like me" (L 481), who has captured the American imagination and who is repeatedly cartooned in a vast array of cultural products.[10]

In a Sunday edition of the *New York Times*, Dickinson critic David Porter's description of what he believes are cartooning scholarly interpretations provides a useful model for understanding how the poet Emily Dickinson is cartooned by some biographies and literary criticism as well as by popular culture. Stating that "now-familiar" feminist critiques tend to render "one-dimensional" interpretations of literary complexities, Porter says that Carolyn Heilbrun reads Lady Macbeth "to represent all females" and judges her analysis "a comparable cartoon of the character, not to mention the female sex" ("Shakespeare Cartoons"). Porter's characterization might just as well describe the relatively one-dimensional image of the poet Emily Dickinson presented in much scholarship. In "Inventing Emily Dickinson" Joyce Van Dyke delineates both the nature of the critical world's enthrallment and the figure with whom even many professional readers have been enthralled: "Attention has focused intently on her personal relationships, and her poetry has frequently been seen as the consequence not of genius, dedication, practice, and revision but as the eruption of a more or less unhappy emotional life. Dickinson is still [in 1984] being described as an artistic ingénue with little intellectual control over her work, the funnel for a poetic production which was a by-product of her personal circumstances rather than the deliberate exercise and fulfillment of extraordinary ability" (277).[11] Or to put it differently, caricature has in most venues superceded the character of determined artist; therefore, when Simon and Garfunkel assure audiences that "She," a future Miss Lonelyheart, reads her Emily Dickinson, while "He," the seriously agonizing young bard, peruses his Robert Frost, they might just as well be describing the majority of scholarly as well as popular culture receptions. No blue-eyed darling Nathaniel, nor swaggering Walt with arm akimbo and hat pulled seductively low, but the seventeen-year-old schoolgirl of the only surviving daguerreotype, the gingerbread-bearing poet of *The Belle of Amherst* enthralled with "Master" and obsessed with renunciation, God, and Father, most often presides over the body of Dickinson's work.

In fairness it must be said that, even though exaggerated, this lovelorn image whose major accomplishment seems to be that she "domesticated heartbreak" does represent one aspect of Dickinson's poetic and epistolary expressions. Yet, as Juhasz, Miller, and I have argued, a single dimension is not the full character. Admittedly, as cartoons ask any reader to suspend certain beliefs, so entertaining the possibility that Dickinson may have been something of a cartoonist requires readers who prefer an exclusively sober-minded poet to suspend prior determinations about who the author was. Entertaining the possibility that she was capable of something akin to cartooning also requires these and similarly minded readers to suspend prior determinations about her intentions. In fact, to discover the poet as cartoonist, of highly visual and comically exaggerated description as well as of sketch and collage, immediately calls this white-clad image of the poet who supposedly never "mastered life" and lived only "after things happen" into question.[12] Her layouts, sketches, letters, and poems are clearly not compulsively or idly produced pastimes, but assertive expressions critiquing conventions of upper-middle-class nineteenth-century American culture. As the following two sections—the first studying some of her layouts and sketches, the second examing her comedic sketches in language—will show, Dickinson's cartoons challenge the literary, political, and family institutions that have helped reproduce the cartoon-like image of a woman poet commodified.

Pictures Sewed to Words

Upon the publication by *Poems by Emily Dickinson* in 1890, Susan Dickinson lamented to William Hayes Ward, editor of the *Independent*, "I have a little article in mind, with illustrations of her [Emily's] own, showing her witty humorous side, which has all been left out of her [Lavinia's] vol. [as Sue chose to call that first edition produced by Higginson and Mabel Loomis Todd]" (H Lowell Autograph).[13] Dickinson's most constant audience, Sue recognized the importance of drawings and cartooning paste-ups to her sister-in-law's artistic objectives. With the exception of a sketch to her brother Austin, all the layouts under study in this section were sent to Sue. In these, Dickinson appears to interrogate the ideology of individual authorship in several ways. At the very least, all of these, like Dickinson's ellipses or gaps in expression, require a reader's collaboration to produce and reproduce meaningful texts, and, with increasing numbers of Dickinson critics, I concur that this strategy is not simply technique, but is also philosophical statement. And I will add that it is one to which Sue was privy. Recognizing that they are bound to arouse audience interest, biographers Martha Dickinson Bianchi and Richard Sewall have printed photographs of her sketches. Many will remember Sewall's reproduction of Dickinson's sketch to John Graves—two tombstones with the caption "In memory of AEolus," the invisible but powerful (and masculine) wind (Sewall 374). Sewall does not comment much on the sketch, calling it Dickinsoniana, but in the context of lifelong poetic production and dedication to her art, perhaps this is a caricature of the dire circumstance, writer's block, and "in memory of poetic inspiration." Or, in a time when male anxiety ran at a feverish pitch worrying about that "damned mob of scribbling women," and when men of letters more sympathetic to women writers like Higginson observed that "during the last half century more books have been written by women and about women than during all the previous uncounted ages" and that the "yearning for a literary career is now almost greater among women than among men" (*Women and the Alphabet* 5,232), perhaps it burlesques the death of the male possession of literature; or, during a time when influential figures like Higginson anxiously observed the "American style of execution, in all high arts" to be "yet hasty and superficial" and exclaimed that Americans needed "the opportunity of high culture somewhere," perhaps the sketch satirizes conventional hierarchies between lofty and low art (Levine 213).[14]

However liberal suffragist Higginson may have been, his ideas about what constitutes important literature were quite conventional and did not extend to concur with Sue that Dickinson's humorous sketches and layouts were significant. His history of American literature, produced after the three volumes of Dickinson's poetry, reveals his staunch beliefs about major and minor literature, high and low culture. There he writes of "concentrating attention on leading figures, instead of burdening the memory with a great many minor names and data," of "pure literature," and of "the highest" and "important" literature and authors (Higginson and Boynton iii, 123).[15] This is important for understanding why he would have deemed Dickinson's cartoons unsuitable for inclusion in the volumes featuring her literature. Since he regarded them as ephemeral products of "feminine" popular culture, Higginson could not imagine how they might serve his presentation of a woman poet concerned with essential truths, sentiments, and finer feelings. For him they would exemplify the "epistolary brilliancy" he readily attributed to women's letters and which he proclaimed must be worked over much more thoroughly in order to be converted "into literature." "The trouble is," Higginson argued, "that into the new [literary] work upon which they [women] are just entering they have not yet brought their thoroughness to bear." Undoubtedly he would argue that, like the poetry collected by Rufus Griswold in *Female Poets of America*, Dickinson's handwritten productions would best be "utterly forgotten" because, presumably dashed off and lacking thoroughness, they have "no root." Though they most assuredly would demonstrate her "cleverness," he would not recognize that such humorous endeavors might teach readers something about the higher aims of her art (*Women and the Alphabet* 229–231).[16] Searching Dickinson's works for the topics contemporarily considered both most important and most marketable—Life, Love, Nature, Time and Eternity—and organizing her lyrics accordingly, these first editors of *Poems by Emily Dickinson* share some assumptions with "serious" critics who devalue and marginalize popular culture.

Analyzing the relative insignificance with which the reproductions of popular culture have been regarded, Andreas Huyssen reminds us of "the notion which gained ground during the nineteenth century that mass culture is somehow associated with woman while real, authentic culture remains the prerogative of men" (47).[17] By editing her poetry and imposing a conventional notion of thoroughness on her work, Higginson and Loomis Todd in one sense sought to elevate the status of the woman poet Dickinson as a producer of lasting culture with roots. However, by grouping her lyrics into topics highlighted in the widely read anthologies of female poetry edited by Rufus Griswold, Caroline May, and Thomas Buchanan Read, Higginson and Loomis Todd also produced a poet more readily bought and sold. But their editions were commodities with pretensions to a cultivated seriousness that inclusion of Dickinson's humorous illustrations might call into question. To take Sue's suggestions and make less conventional editions of her poetry "showing her witty humorous side" would have meant including items believed to be products of "low," dispensable, parlor culture inconsequential to weighty literary objectives. In contrast to their opinion, Sue apparently judged the distinction between "high" and "low" invidious, as do feminists and many other critics today. In fact, her brief critique is a precursor of Barton St. Armand's recent assertion that the "art of assemblage" or "'quilting' of elite and popular ideas onto a sturdy folk form, frame, or fabric" is paradigmatical for Dickinson's poetic designs and the range of her comic expressions (9–10).

Since the layouts and sketches, handmade greeting cards, scrapbooks, and herbariums (collections or "books" of dried plant specimens mounted and systematically arranged for reference) fashioned by so many women of Dickinson's class were regarded by editors like Higginson as clever products hastily made and not as items for serious study, they were treated as if they would undermine important critical goals.[18] Of course the threat of mass culture, "against which high art has to shore up its terrain," is that one will be seduced into enacting Marx's nightmare, lose oneself in delusions and daydreams, and thus become primarily a passive consumer and not an active producer involved with the complex pleasures offered by "high" art (Huyssen 56).[19] Similarly, the detraction from deliberative study that Higginson surely assumed the layouts and sketches posed is that they offer merely an occasion for consumption but not for critical engagement, that they tell us a bit about Dickinson's personal pleasures but very little about her artistic designs and literary processes. That miscalculation proved profound, for writerly participations on the part of readers are precisely what they require.

When Dickinson produced her cutouts, she did not turn to shopping catalogs and popular magazines so much as she turned to her Bible, her *New England Primer*, and her father's Dickens, texts considered on the one hand sacred and, on the other, inviolable as literary entertainment and guides to proper speech. To observe only that these mutilations of her Bible or of Dickens or of a guide for using language properly are irreverent misses the more important points to be made about them, for these manipulations of texts are transformations, opportunities for Emily Dickinson and her readers to exert control over expression by remaking sup-

posedly fixed utterances and thereby challenge conventional authorities in
a constructive way. By manipulating the material embodiments of texts,
Dickinson clowns and toys with convention, and thereby overturns the
dicta of her day. Careful examination of four layouts and sketches reveals
how she critically exposes five different types of cultural authority by "cartooning": that of poetic tradition, that of patriotism, that of romantic
thralldom, that of the patriarchal family, and that established by the rigidities of the printing press.

The first layout to consider is also the simplest: atop "Whose cheek is
this?" (H B 186; P 82), Dickinson attached a cutout of a robin from her
New England Primer.

The poem reads:

> Whose cheek is this?
> What rosy face
> Has lost a blush today?
> I found her ‚ 'pleiad' ‚ in the woods
> And bore her safe away.
>
> Robins, in the tradition
> Did cover such with leaves,
> But which the Cheek –
> And which the pall
> *My* scrutiny deceives

When she sent this poem to Sue, Dickinson sewed or pinned a flower
just to the right of the cutout of the robin glued onto this page (or leaf),
and the questions comprising the first three lines of the poem refer
to that wilting token. The "rescue" of this little star of the woods is to a
"safety" of death; it will be preserved, but not as ebullient, colorful, and
full of life. In preservation the flower "Has lost a blush," is dried and
withered in decease. The robins "in the tradition" are the versifying
multitudes covering real life by writing the many "leaves," pages upon
pages, about nature, love, life, God, time and eternity, the popular topics
for last century's American poetry. Especially when one keeps in mind the
wide circulation of Fanny Fern's *Fern Leaves from Fanny's Portfolio* (1853)
and its probable influence on Whitman's producing *Leaves of Grass* (1855),
Dickinson's pun is obvious.[20] The query of the last three lines—is poetry killing life into art or giving some semblance of life a new lease on
existence—either deceives the speaker or is a question the speaker scruti-
nizes and regards, perhaps because of its overly simple dichotomies, as deceptive. Like the flower attached to the page, poems idolized wither and die.

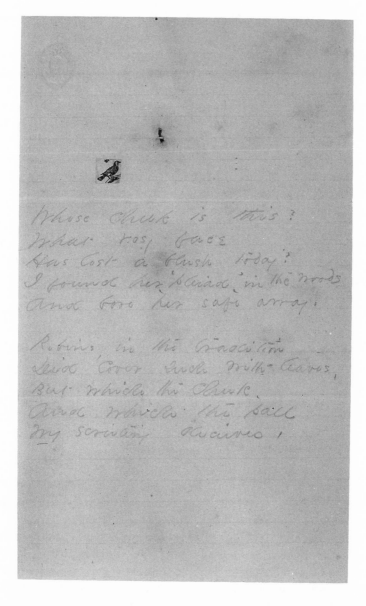

Copy of "Whose cheek is this?" sent to Sue. By permission of the Houghton Library, Harvard University.

Why are the visual props important, and what purpose do they serve? The dying flower makes a three-dimensional cartoon as it helps to clarify the reference of the pronoun "this." The cutout of the robin seems superfluous, yet its significations are not merely decorative. Most likely, Sue would have recognized the snippet as one from the *New England Primer*. Importantly, Dickinson situates the grammar book cutout so the robin faces the flower or pleiad. Since "pleiad" may also refer to the seven tragic poets of Alexandria, perhaps the lyric with layout is designed to suggest that the robins "in the tradition," or the poetesses "extricating humanity from some hopeless ditch" (L 380), make elementary or grammar book sense of tragic poetry. Clearly the layout and attachment function as commentary on the poem, and the reader must develop their intertextual connotations. Doing so, one cannot help but recognize nor resist being amused by Dickinson's caricature of nineteenth-century popular poetry. Dressed up with a souvenir from nature's bounty and a woodcut of a warbling thrush commonly associated with merry times, what appears to be a relatively insignificant ditty of a lyric in fact mirthfully interrogates common poetic praxis.

Such implicit demands on the reader are evident in her other illustrations. A sketch incorporated into a letter to her brother in the early 1850s lampoons Congress, particularly the Whigs (her father's party), hence privately to Austin pasquinades patriotic duty. The rather conservative Edward Dickinson was a member of the House of Representatives, but his eldest daughter used his official stationery liberally when she wrote her brother. The poet draws around the diminutive embossed likeness of the U.S. Capitol building, adding a smokestack to its dome and, on its left, a little stick figure shuffling along. Beneath the cartoon is the caption, "Member from 10*th*!" Thomas H. Johnson describes this sketch in a brief editorial note, interpreting it as "a striding Indian" in feathered headdress approaching the smoking dome. Indeed, the little figure has something sticking straight up off his head, but it is not plainly a headdress. Since he was a Whig (and it was a dying party), and since his frustrations with Washington were no secret, Dickinson might well be depicting her exasperated father with his hair standing on end—or "flipping his wig"—as he approaches the house of government. Whatever one's interpretation, her humor is obvious. As Katharine Zadravec has noted, the poet "is satirizing her congressman father's arrival in Washington" (27).

This is very much in keeping with and lends credibility to a story her niece told about Aunt Emily's visit to Washington while her father served in Congress:

Enlargement of stick figure:

(A 617; L 144)[21]

Copy of cartoon satirizing their congressman father's arrival in Washington sent to Austin. By permission of the Trustees of Amherst College.

She had a keen scent for the meanings hid beneath the goodly outside of diplomacy and watched for developments in home and foreign
policies with surprising acumen. The winter she was at Willard's, during her Father's congressional career, she is said to have astonished his
political friends by her insight and created quite a sensation by her
wit, though the only story I recall now was of her saying to a prim old
Chief Justice of the Supremest sort, when the plum pudding on fire
was offered—"Oh Sir, may one eat of hell fire with impunity here?"
(Bianchi xiii–xiv)

The wry query reflects a sensibility similar to that evident in the presumably shocked figure approaching the smokestack-adorned capitol. Sister
Lavinia's somewhat lighthearted account of Mr. Dickinson's arrival in
Washington complements Emily's sketch. According to Vinnie, a man accustomed to enjoying power over almost all of his neighbors in Amherst
felt a little intimidated in the halls of Congress: "He told us in his last
letter, that he had been sending out his cards to various persons of rank.
He says he dont know much about etiquet but is trying to learn [*sic*]"
(Bingham, *Home* 329). Both Emily's drawing and the anecdote about her
visit to the District of Columbia evince efforts on the daughter's part to
put a humorous spin on what were by all accounts frustrating times for
her father and anxious times for a family concerned for him. What could
have been dreary concerned responses are instead comically deflating jabs
at pompous politicos. By engaging in these kinds of epistolary and dinner-
time repartee, she challenges blind belief in and obeisance to provincial
institutions like the government of these United States.

Twenty-five years later Dickinson was breezy but unequivocal when to
Abigail Cooper she remarked upon her alienation from the officially delineated nation:

"My Country, 'tis of thee," has always meant the Woods – to me –
"Sweet Land of Liberty," I trust is your own –   (L 509, about 1877)

A few years after that irreverent note, she, with considerable levity, was
even more forthright about her feeling for patriotism and Fatherland in a
letter to Elizabeth Holland:

"George Washington was the Father of his Country" – "George
Who?"
That sums all Politics to me – but then I love the Drums, and they
are busy now –   (L 950, late autumn 1884)

The United States is "their" and "his" country, never Dickinson's, and it is the sound of patriotic pageantry, of men in unison, not its sense, that amuses and/or attracts her. Likewise, July 4th is a holiday when "Little Boys are commemorating the advent of their Country" (L 650, July 1880). As she had more than twenty years earlier, through ironic deflation, Dickinson mocks the heromaking institutions of men, governments, and their armies. These sociopolitical commentaries are all the more startling to today's reader since they come from a poet about whom it is a commonplace to say that "she all but ignored the stirring events of her time," that she cared not a whit for national causes, and was "never discursive on historical matters" (Sewall 535, 445). Through these comic portrayals readers can clearly see that Dickinson had not just a moment's but several decades worth of doubts about the American democratic process. But as Nancy Walker observes, for Dickinson, "the expression of freedom was laughter" and wit "provides the detachment from convention which allows her an identity separate" from that which customary religious, social, and political commitments "would demand" ("Emily Dickinson and the Self" 63). Whether because the received biographies render her as apolitical, or because she has been considered more witty and ironic than boldly humorous and comic, or for some other reason distorting literary historiography, her challenges to the official political institutions of her time have not been descried. When the point of Dickinson's humor, "her usual means of declaring independence," has been similarly overlooked or her topic misconstrued, her interrogation of other powerful cultural or social institutions has likewise hardly been noticed (Walker, "Emily Dickinson and the Self" 63).

Interpreting "A poor – torn Heart – a tattered heart – / That sat it down to rest," (H B 175; P 78), some have argued that this poem was written about the same time as the infamous "Master" letters, and so is yet another testament to Dickinson's unrequited dejection and thralldom to romantic love and her desire to join the ranks of those ensconced in the institution of marriage. Indeed, the handwriting does match that of the penciled "Master" draft beginning "Oh' did I offend it" (A 829, 829a; L 248).[22] Yet the two pictures Dickinson clipped from her father's copy of Dickens' *The Old Curiosity Shop* suggest anything but interpretation without irony. In fact, by making a "cartoon" of what has been judged to be one of her most sentimental lyrics, she arguably critiques the one-dimensional, cartoon-like quality of nineteenth-century notions relegating women to a "separate sexual caste" and defining females exclusively by their relationships to love.[23] If the speaker voices her grief, she has become able to joke about it, is in control, not driven out of control and into effusive, unreflective expression.

The poems reads:

A poor – torn Heart – a tattered heart,
That sat it down to rest ,
Nor noticed that the Ebbing Day
Flowed silver to the West,
Nor noticed night did soft descend,
Nor Constellation burn ,
Intent upon a vision
Of Latitudes unknown ,

The Angels, happening that way
This dusty heart espied ,
Tenderly took it up from toil,
And carried it to God ,
There – Sandals for the Barefoot ,
There – gathered from the gales
Do the blue Havens by the hand
Lead the wandering sails.

When Dickinson sent this poem next door to her sister-in-law, she appended a picture of Little Nell being comforted by her grandfather to the top of the poem with pink thread; then, also with pink thread, she bound a cutout of Little Nell being ferried to heaven by a host of angels to the bottom of the poem. This appears to have been attached in such a way so that when the missive was unfolded, the bottom picture of Little Nell among the seraphs popped up—like a pop-up greeting card—to the reader. In this context calling attention to her appropriation of Dickens' work and the poem's hyperbolic overstatement, a lyric that might be either disregarded or read earnestly as religious or romantic sentiment becomes the cartooning play of one writer responding to another.[24] The fact that her own surname christened her "Dickens' son" was surely not lost on this writer so given to puns and verbal play. What is also clear from Dickinson making this poem in direct response to Dickens and then sending it to Sue is the women's communion and mutual play as readers, kinds of interpretive interaction common among America's literate classes.

As Cathy Davidson has pointed out after examining the responses of earlier nineteenth-century American readers, in their "inscriptions, the marginalia, and even the physical condition of surviving copies of early American novels" twentieth-century readers encounter century-old,

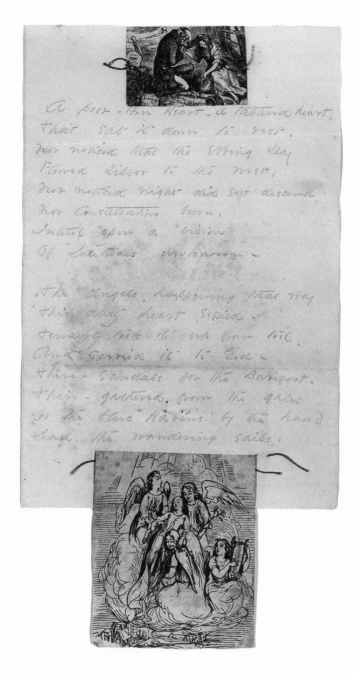

Copy of "A poor–torn Heart" sent to Sue. By permission of the Houghton Library, Harvard University.

seemingly extemporaneous poems written to instruct borrowers about how to treat a particular copy of a book, poems of reverie about a novel's character, and poems inscribed in response to a novel's especially emotional passages. Commentaries on a novel's moral or entertainment value are also evident, and in a copy of *Charlotte Temple* one reader even doodled a rendition of the heroine. Besides revealing "a surprising range of reader response" and books prized for decades by the same reader or group of readers, some names and inscriptions in books begin "to suggest the outlines of a contemporaneous interpretive community"—books passed back and forth between siblings, friends, acquaintances, and bequeathed to subsequent generations (75–79). Dickinson's production of "A poor – torn Heart – a tattered heart" for Sue is part of that genteel world of reader response.

Dickinson's cartooning cutout works to undercut any culturally predetermined insistence that hers is simply a reiterative poem articulating Little Nell's miserable flight into angelic rescue. What might be read all too solemnly when divorced from the illustrations Dickinson attached cannot be read without humor with her original context restored. What is unusual about Emily Dickinson's act is that she does not limit herself to the borders of leaves or back pages of *The Old Curiosity Shop* itself as do the readers of Susanna Rowson's *Charlotte Temple*, *A Spelling Dictionary*, and Samuel Relf's *Infidelity, or the Victims of Sentiment* whom Davidson describes. Instead of situating her poetic commentary on the Dickensian scenes so that it is marginal, Dickinson scissors illustrations originally bound into the novel and, by attaching them to her poem, subordinates the printed text to her holographic response. The poet's production invites readers to peruse both the poem and Dickens' story again, reading them "backward," against conventional instructions, lest "the plunge from the front overturn" sense (PF 30).[25] Reading straightforwardly, without admitting any role for a sense of humor, produces a kind of nonsense by consigning Little Nell and female characters similarly fated to only one sort of fortune and their readers to facile responses that either mawkishly identify with or cynically explain away such scenes. In this conventional scheme of things, failures of authorial and readerly imaginations prevail.

Dickinson's reformulation, on the other hand, both evinces and demands imaginative interpretation. By cutting up Dickens' novel, Dickinson demonstrates that no plot is fixed. By attaching illustrations included in *The Old Curiosity Shop* to a poem superficially reiterative of the novel's sentiments, she invites readers to consider how heavy-handed and gratuitous Dickens and/or his publisher chose to be. Most important, by re-

moving the illustrations from the context of the novel itself and attaching
them to a seemingly simple lyric in which the rhythms and rhymes are
subtly unsettled, Dickinson encourages readers to peruse beyond the predictable responses. Scanning the poem, a reader's conventional expectations for an iambic tetrameter line are immediately disrupted by a spon-
daic second foot in the first line. To begin the poem with such heavy
syllabic emphasis ironically attentuates any straightforward tone by over-
stressing both the pathetic singularity of and the rending infliction to "A
poor – torn Heart." More suggestively, the first stanza's regularly alter-
nating tetrameter, trimeter iambic lines are broken in the seventh by the
three-and-a-half-foot "Intent upon a vision," unless, of course, the reader
enunciates the last word out of its two-syllable modern English—*vizh-
ən*—and back into some bastardized three-syllable rendition—*vizh-e-ən*—
pretentiously informed by its Middle English and Old French origins. In
the second stanza, a three-and-a-half-foot fifth line appears where one
expects a four foot line in "There – Sandals for the Barefoot." Amusingly,
the extra syllable is "-foot," left bare of its iambic companion. As Paul
Fussell has observed, "poetic meter is a prime physical and emotional con-
stituent of poetic meaning (13)."[26] By over- and understating meter, then,
Dickinson urges her readers to inflect the poem with far more than sen-
timentally sober-minded tones. The death of Little Nell also prompted
Oscar Wilde, half a century later, to encourage readers to interpret imaginatively and well beyond convention when he remarked that one must
have a heart of stone to read about it without bursting out laughing.

The special effects of Dickinson's cartooning strategies here are not
those of an elitism that would belittle readers moved by such scenes as the
death of Little Nell. Instead, by mixing media—illustrations from a popular novel with linguistic descriptions of brokenhearted, barefooted, and
angelic figures common in popular poetry—Dickinson also mixes tones
and in doing so reminds audiences that no singleminded or singlehearted
response to a subject is enough. Dickinson's strength as an artist in this
instance is akin to the important service Richard Poirier ascribed to the
work of the Beatles: "they locate the beauty and pathos of commonplace
feelings even while they work havoc with fashionable or tiresome expressions of these feelings" (124). Dickinson's ironic commentary simultaneously remarks upon reading her lyric, Dickens' novel, and the myriad lyrics of "secret sorrow" permeating her culture, as well as upon critical
attitudes that would dismiss them all in the name of a hierarchy of proper
interests. Implicitly the poem as Dickinson wrote and presented it to Sue
challenges the literary cliché of the lovelorn lady, as represented in forms

as diverse as Clarissa Harlowe to Emmy pining for Captain Dobbin to Higginson's "virgin recluse." Thus challenging the preconceptions of literary institutions, she eludes a critical control that would classify her as a particular kind of poet; similarly, her works complicated the categorizations of Higginson and Loomis Todd and had to be pruned and rearranged, sometimes dramatically, to fit into them, as when they scissored away the last two stanzas of Dickinson's sardonically bold "A solemn thing – it was – / I said – / A woman – white – to be" (F 14; P 271) to produce a conventionally celebratory bridal tribute, "Wedded."[27]

Apparently, Dickinson also eluded the controlling designs of her father. When she stays too late next door at an Evergreens' fete, she pokes fun at his reprimand by sending a cartooning cutout over to Sue the next morning.

The text of the note is as follows:

> My "position"!
> Cole,

> P.S. – Lest you misapprehend,
> the unfortunate insect upon
> the *left* is Myself, while the
> Reptile upon the *right* ˎ is my
> more immediate friends, and
> connections.
>   As Ever,
>   Cole,

Clipped from her *New England Primer* is the illustration for the moral lesson "Young Timothy / Learnt sin to fly." The cartoon "shows a youth pursued by an upright wolf" or dragon-like "creature with forked tail," and is signed "Cole" (H B 114; L 214). "To the note" Thomas Johnson found "another attached by Mrs. Bianchi: 'Sent over the morning after a revel—when my Grandfather with his lantern appeared suddenly to take Emily home the hour nearing indecent midnight' " (L 214 n.; see also Bianchi, *Life and Letters* 156). Most likely this signature refers to the English painter of American landscapes, Thomas Cole, and more specifically to Bryant's poem, "To Cole, the Painter, Departing for Europe," which beseeches Cole to carry a "living image" of America with him. The poem concludes: "Keep that earlier, wilder image [of America] bright." Dickinson's recollection of the revel the night before is certainly "wilder" than the company of her father. By naming herself Cole and subtly alluding to

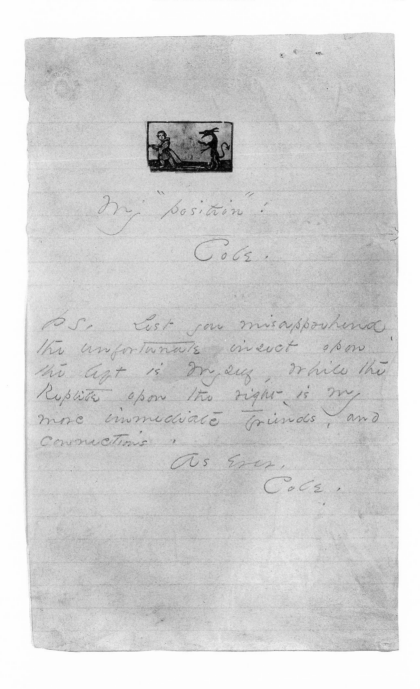

Copy of "My 'position'!" sent to Sue. By permission of the Houghton Library, Harvard University.

Bryant, Dickinson both authorizes her complaint by aligning herself and her friends with some of the most respected figures of the day and demonstrates her good-humored reception of her father's overbearing reprimand through the jollity conveyed by such a ludicrous comparison. In light of her father's disapproval, her lighthearted sanguine response is further conveyed by the fact that she represents herself as one of the little beasts almost universally received as pests and depicts her friends as mythical reptilian creatures frequently associated with obstacles to be battled and overcome to complete successful quests. Her father's retrieval of his eldest daughter from an evening of sociability and fun is thus compared to a heroic venture in this clipping and note that form a cartoon both to make light of his scolding and simultaneously to proclaim Dickinson's affection for the revelers. This playful challenge to patriarchal authority that seems too possessive is not bitter or spiteful, but "makes room for Daddy"; she pokes fun at prim and conventional manners which leave little room for spontaneity, but she does so without acrimony.

There was much that Dickinson could not command about her situation, but she could and did govern her outlook. Recognizing the bold cartooning humor of a woman whose wit has been characterized as understated shakes up assumptions about how precisely literary history has rendered Emily Dickinson. Her privatized role and productions as cartoonist raise many questions about genre, about editing as interpretation and the role of textual reproduction in shaping an author's biography, and about the critical relation of these editorially obscured documents to her poems, letters, and letter-poems, as well as to literature and texts in general. What is plain is that Dickinson takes often empty social forms—the role of friendly neighbor forwarding a flower, the role of fellow reader sharing a ditty about a sobbing character, the role of satisfied guest sending a thank-you note for a riotous evening the night before, and, as we shall see in the next section, the indulgent or comforting role of maiden aunt—and rescues these from the banal by turning them into artistic performances, occasions for displaying her warmth, her wit, her respect for and encouragement of readers.

. . . but a Few Words Can Make a Picture

Long translated into forms mass-reproducible, Dickinson's linguistic "cartooning" has been readily available to her readers. More important, however, her highly visual, humorous portrayals in language sketches complement understandings of the layouts and drawings and further critical appreciations of the range of her literary project. Dickinson's verbal descriptions of family figures, nature's figures, political figures, and heavenly figures often focus on one characteristic to caricature an institution or person, while configurations of portrayals in her poems, letters, and letter-poems into several- (usually four-) part segments may remind today's reader of the ways in which stories are relayed by panels in a cartoon strip. Dickinson and her contemporaries would associate such pictorial progressions with storytelling series of paintings like Cole's *The Course of Empire* or *The Voyage of Life* or like Hogarth's *The Harlot's Progress*, *The Rake's Progress*, and *Marriage à la Mode* popularized through widely distributed engravings; or perhaps their associations would even have been with literary responses to stories woven into medieval tapestries like that by Spenser relating the tale of Venus and Adonis via description of the tapestry of "rare device, and wondrous wit" hanging on Malecasta's castle wall (*The Faerie Queene* III.i.34).

As St. Armand and Judith Farr have recently noted, Dickinson's appreciations for paintings and the influence of such aesthetic sensibilities on her poetic art have been insufficiently examined. The Evergreens, Austin and Sue's Italianate villa next door, was a showcase boasting an impressive collection of art objects, especially paintings. St. Armand observes that in poems like "They called me to the / Window, for / 'twas Sunset' – Some one / said" (F 26; P 628), Dickinson "boldly . . . transfers" the conventional subject matter of John F. Kensett's painting *Sunset with Cows* "momentarily to the realm of cloud" (282).[28] Mimicking Kensett's brilliantly vivid portrayal of a river scene at dusk in which a few pink, gold, orange, and indigo clouds compose the top portion of the canvas while a lone figure shepherds ten or so cows through the dark greenish-black bottom third of the painting, Dickinson's poem features a "Sapphire Farm" with "Opal Cattle." Significantly, her pastoral figures are located in the sky instead of by a stream and dissolve into "Ships," the "Decks" of which are vast enough "to seat the / Skies." On second glance, these visions also dissolve or are "rubbed away" by a "Showman" who, like the poet herself, transposes the conventional into the sublime through startling juxtapositions and unanticipated translocations. The poem's "Showman" teases its speaker by obliterating the fantastic vision and the speaker likewise teases the reader by claiming that the "Farm," "Opal Herd," and "Mediterranean," all mentioned in the final stanza, are in fact not there. St. Armand recovers yet another aspect of Dickinson appropriating techniques from other media and, in doing so, reveals the fact that her creative, always active habit of mind led her both literally to cut up printed works and thereby reformulate texts and figuratively to cut out subject matter and techniques of other artists in order to extend and enhance her own strategies. Similar to the "bold transfer" St. Armand discovers in "They called me to the / Window, for" and the reconstitutions in her layouts and sketches reviewed earlier in this chapter, her language cartoons display transformative expressions that realign supposedly stable relationships of people, places, and things to the world.

Since they depend entirely on words to make the illustrations, the pictorial verbal arrangements rendered as examples in this section are of course quite different from the drawings readers encounter daily in the newspaper. Yet, through their ludicrously comic portrayals and humorous "mini-series," these letters and poems evince a kind of "cartooning." As if jocularly responding to and revising Sidney's declaration about a poet's work, Dickinson time and again produces "speaking pictures." Throughout the letters, readers discover highly visual, hyperbolic, "snapshot" descriptions similar to the single frame cartoons featured in nineteenth-century America's *Harper's* and *Frank Leslie's Illustrated Newspaper*, while in some of the poems readers find a series of vignettes similar to the narrative frames of a Cole or Hogarth series. Thus examining her comic strategies in a well-known reported incident and in a few letters as well as in a century-long favorite poem and one frequently recycled in the last couple of decades of criticism adduces some of her briefly narrative, grossly exaggerated, surprisingly humorous lyric strategies as cartooning elements. By revealing more about Dickinson's demanding attitudes that require readers' thoughtful participations, such study also elaborates Constance Rourke's and Nancy Walker's claims that Emily Dickinson was "in a profound sense a comic poet" (Walker, "Emily Dickinson and the Self" 57).[29] Accounts of delightful, intense visual productions and cartooning sensibility characterize many of the apocryphal stories about her interactions with relatives and friends. For example, as Sandra Gilbert and others have noted, the "Uncle Emily" of the following well-known anecdote routinely transforms the daily and domestic into the wondrous and magical ("The Wayward Nun" 39). Her neighbor Clara Newman Turner remembered:

> [Emily's] nephew [Ned], boy-like, had a way of leaving anything superfluous to his immediate needs at Grandma's. After one of these little "Sins of Omission," over came his high-top boots, standing erect and spotless on a silver tray, their tops running over with Emily's flowers. At another time the little overcoat was returned with each velvet pocket pinned down, and a card with "*Come in*" on one, and "*Knock*" on the other. The "Come in" proved to be raisins; the "Knock," cracked nuts.   (Leyda 2:481)

With but a few words, Dickinson makes a picture for her nephew; out of the materials and situation immediately at hand, she produces a three-dimensional cartoon like the flower pinned to "Whose cheek is this?" She does not merely return Ned's overcoat, but, flexing her creative muscle, makes a delightful occasion of doing so even as she demands that Ned be an active, participatory reader: if he refuses to engage this text, he will remain *un*rewarded by raisins and nuts.

In a similar vein, when Ned was stung by a hornet, she writes a cheering note:

Dear Ned –
    You know I never liked you in those Yellow Jackets. (L 511,
July 1877)

Analyzing how this deceptively simple pun works, a reader identifies her own several complex performances: she recognizes immediately that, with hornets or yellow jackets metonymically identified with the slightly jaundiced evidence of their stings and represented as garish overcoats, the preference to alleviate a loved one's minor pain is represented as a matter of taste, thus as something that can be, like a tacky jacket, thrown off at will. In both these, Dickinson retains a couple of positions at once—as playful aunt, and, as playful author for a split instant at one with her reader when they share humorous perspective. The pleasures offered by these humorous texts depend on a reader's "getting" the joke. More obviously than almost any poetic text, a joke explicitly requires listener/reader participation. As we observed in the opening chapter, the joke provokes laughter only if it is delivered to (i.e., recognized by) the listener/reader; unless it is shared, the joke is not a joke. No critic can pretend, as was standard for critics who overextended the comparison of a poem to a painting or sculpture, that the pleasures of a joke are delivered like those of an art object, that a joke is a finely chiseled or decorated piece, an entity unto itself waiting like an urn to be appreciated. While art objects are likely to be damaged in handling and viewers are instructed to keep their distance, jokes (and poems) invite listener/readers to come close and in the act of listening/reading join the production and reproduction of texts. The appeals and demands of Dickinson's jokes parallel those made by her literary texts. As both her demands upon readers and treatment of the printed works or the artifacts or "fragment(s) of substance, occupying a part of the space of books" found in the Dickinson family library show, the most important texts are those co-produced by the reader. To a significant degree she anticipates Roland Barthes' claim that texts are "meth-odological fields" which can be *"experienced only in an activity of production"* (an act of interpretation, for example) (*Image—Music—Text* 156–157). Clearly, static printed works were not sacred to her as objects but were valued as texts available for her readerly and authorial reformulations.

At the very least, a poem or a joke is a duet, even when the audience is the author at a later time, for as soon as she begins to write, the author becomes audience, too. Without this dialogue between author and audi-ence, humor's effects—which turn the world topsy-turvy—could neither be delivered nor received. Recognition of the importance Dickinson atta-ches to dialogic textual encounters is vital for study of the poet so often labeled "solipsistic," withdrawn, not so much concerned with others as with herself, nor with communication as with dictating the terms of verbal expression. This intentional, self-conscious play by Dickinson is not lim-ited to the audience of her nephew or Sue, but she clowned often, plying every opportunity to remake quotidian experience. In another deceptively simple cartooning epistolary moment, Dickinson substantiates Gary Lee Stonum's recent claim that "nearly all of her remarks about poetry [and writing] in letters, poems, or recorded conversation imagine literature from the point of view of the audience" (10):

> That was a lovely letter of Fanny's. It put the cat to playing and the kettle to purring, and two or three birds in plush teams reined nearer to the window. . . . (L 375, 27 July 1872)

Kettles purring and birds behaving as if they are steeds pulling a coach are depictions not bound by the realistic or the probable, and ones that implicitly ask the reader to indulge in the pleasures afforded by her own imagination. To compliment cousin Fanny Norcross' writing, then, Dick-inson offers exaggerated visual descriptions of the effects of the former's letters that, attempting to delight by return mail, also complement her own pleasure as audience by reciprocally extending it to her addressees.

When Dickinson describes the joys of her conservatory to Elizabeth Holland, she exclaims, "My flowers are near and foreign, and I have but to cross the floor to stand in the Spice Isles," then elaborates her experi-ence of the day in an even more cartoon-like fashion: "The Wind blows gay today and the Jays bark like Blue Terriers" (L 315, early March 1866). Winds roaring with laughter and birds that bark are characters today's readers expect to encounter in the funny papers and that Dickinson's con-temporaries might have expected from one of the illustrated weeklies or from a writer given to Dickensian twists animating the inanimate and transmogrifying the natural order.[30] In an earlier letter to the Hollands, Dickinson recounts articles in the local newspaper, the *Republican*, as if it were a funny paper, whatever its editors (of whom Holland was one) intended. Bloodily devastating experiences are translated into cartoon-like stories:

> Who writes those funny accidents, where railroads meet each other unexpectedly, and gentlemen in factories get their heads cut off informally? The author, too, relates them in such a sprightly way, that they are quite attractive. Vinnie was disappointed to-night, that there were not more accidents – I read the news aloud, while Vinnie was sewing. . . . (L 133, autumn 1853)

Framing a horrible event by picturing it in words that conjure comic images defends against its gory significance, relieving readers even while informing them. But such depictions can also jade audiences to harsh realities. Here, in humorous appropriation of the kind of observations made by her contemporary Rebecca Harding Davis, years before Norris or Sinclair and more than a century before world wars and, later, televised wars, Dickinson describes a world made comically and insensitively surreal by styles of journalism. As a reader she claims to take pleasure in the giddy writing and seems empathetically immunized to the fatalities. But she is careful to point out that it is the cartoon-like writing, not the event itself, that delights her. Humorously translated, the occurrence is both less and more horrifying to her as she implicitly critiques the often callous reportage of journalism when limbs and lives lost and even decapitation are reduced to a few "objective" paragraphs.

The linguistic cartoons discussed so far caricature supposedly negligible routines of daily life and, in doing so, turn them into happy, memorable events; or, as in the last example, Dickinson's cartoon critiques the effects when mass-marketed information transforms calamities into fodder for storytelling. In reflecting upon them, readers see Dickinson's preoccupation with audience—both herself and other readers. Both caricature and jovially holding up to ridicule are most often associated with political cartoons, for they allow critics to lessen the offensiveness of negative commentaries and keep the political system intact by delivering them through a joke. Thus cartoons translate even scathing criticisms into socially permissible statements. If "witticisms" are indeed "the simultaneous preservation of the ego and the socialization of psychic activity" (Kristeva 227),[31] then the following linguistic cartoon provides Dickinson the opportunity to criticize a relative rather sharply without completely disrupting the political system of the family, to turn a potentially alienating remark topsy-turvy and make it sociable:

> [Aunt] L[ibbie] goes to Sunderland, Wednesday, for a minute or two; leaves here at 6 1/2—what a fitting hour—and will breakfast the night before; such a smart atmosphere! The trees stand right up straight when they hear her boots, and will bear crockery wares instead of fruit, I fear. She hasn't starched the geraniums yet, but will have ample time, unless she leaves before April. Emily is very mean, and her children in dark mustn't remember what she says about damsel. (L 286, mid-October 1863)

Sarcastically, Dickinson draws an aunt so cleverly well-prepared that she eats her breakfast the night before. With characteristic hyperbole, Dickinson imagines that, to maintain a perfect appearance for this most severe of judges, even the trees will put on artificial, apparently flawless, ceramic fruit, which can be smashed and broken but never eaten and enjoyed. Life with Libbie is, therefore, a long way from Eden. Since Aunt Libbie expects everything to be perfectly arranged, all property "straight[ened]," and every endeavor abandoned in order to take leave of or greet her, Dickinson elsewhere remarks that all stand "erect and smart" (L 331) in anticipation, as if called to attention and for inspection by "the only male relative on the female side," whose visits have the "flavor of court-martial" (L 473).

Though Dickinson cannot resist poking fun at her aunt's prim and conventional manners and lack of spontaneity, her self-conscious last sentence reveals her awareness that laughter is an act of aggression, lifting "inhibitions by breaking through prohibitions" (Kristeva 224). Since laughter tends to turn the world upside down, messages which would otherwise probably never be received and which one would most likely not want to send can be conveyed with jesting jibe, for in humorous discourse conventional, sober expectations do not apply. In spite of her ostensible self-consciousness about criticizing her aunt, Dickinson writes the less than flattering commentary anyway.

Apparently recognizing its social power, when Dickinson comments on play or on laughter, she allies both with holy callings. Of play, she remarks to the cousins Norcross:

> Blessed are they that play, for theirs is the kingdom of heaven.
> (L 690, early spring 1881)

Making a Blakean move in revisionary mythmaking, Dickinson offers her readers the lighter side of *The Marriage of Heaven and Hell* by adding a beatitude noticeably missing from Jesus' grave dicta. In a more subtle move, she uses an image of a bird so often used to represent poets, especially those nineteenth-century women singing because of their "secret sorrow," to praise her close friend Elizabeth Holland for her gift of laughter:

> I can always rely on your little Laugh, which is what the Essayist calls "the immortal Peewee." (L 692, spring 1881)

The essayist is Higginson, the essay "The Life of Birds" in the *Atlantic Monthly*, and a peewee any one of several small birds. In her study of American women poets before 1900, Cheryl Walker observes that Anne Bradstreet's "Contemplations" climaxes when "the poet is attracted by the song of Philomel, the female bird of poetry," that "during the colonial period 'Philomela' was used as a pseudonym for several women poets," and that "from the very beginning this women's tradition in American poetry has been a nightingale tradition, bound up with themes of aspiration and frustrated longing" (15). That Dickinson was conscious of this tradition has been frequently discussed and continually publicized since her closest contemporary, Sue, wrote, "If a nightingale sings with her breast against a thorn, why not *we*?" (H Box 8). Here Sue reinscribes the image of the nineteenth-century poetess we all know best: she who feels intensely, knows suffering no one else knows, and writes as a result. When Dickinson names Elizabeth Holland "the immortal Peewee" in honor of her reliable "little Laugh," then, she overlays the image of passionate private painful feeling so often attributed to women with gaiety, thus revises conventional poetic symbology to articulate her delight in a friend.

Intriguingly, though Holland's religious beliefs and more somber side have often been discussed, it is Annie Holland, Elizabeth and Josiah's daughter, who overlays the overemphasized anecdotes depicting an always withdrawn Emily Dickinson with a story about her sociability. To Martha Dickinson Bianchi, Dickinson's niece, she writes:

> When I was a young girl visiting in Amherst I went to a Reception in your grandparents [*sic*] house, and met your Aunt Emily. She was so surrounded by people that I had no chance to talk with her, and she asked me to call on her the next morning. (Leyda 2:115)

Holland goes on to describe their next day's meeting. She was offered wine or a rose, and though she could not recall the specifics of their conversation, Holland did remember that "[Emily's] voice, her looks, and her whole personality made an impression on me that is still very vivid after all these years." At the center of the party in this story, and in sharp contrast to the weird woman out in the hall or up in her room frequently replicated in scholarship and in popular culture, auburn-haired Emily Dickinson appears to be friendly and sociable instead of timid and neurotically secluded. In fact, humor is sociable, tending to bring author and reader together. To laugh together is to be in sync—at least for a moment. Humor tends to be a friendly way of looking at the world. Humor is a way of accessing power, of maintaining playful, symbolic mastery. When one delivers a joke, witticism, or comic story and makes readers giggle, the teller seems in control of audience response and the audience feels privy to a special exchange. As recognition of Dickinson as funny and friendly challenges the cycle of reception that time and again simplifies matters of interpretation by reproducing almost exclusively the stories of the recluse, and as Dickinson challenges the image of the female bird singing from frustration and/or sorrow, so in one of her most famous poems Dickinson, through revisionary representations, simultaneously challenges easy conclusions about the significations of rituals of the suitor and of the undertaker.[32]

Perhaps her most widely anthologized poem, "Because I could not / stop for Death – " (F 23; P 712) was one of those on which Allen Tate and Ivor Winters focused their critical energies when their studies "helped retrieve Dickinson's poetry from obscurity" (Galperin 63).[33] Though often used to show that many of Dickinson's lyrics can be sung to the melody of "The Yellow Rose of Texas," and though its Dickensian exaggerations in description suggest that comedic connotations are perhaps feasible, even the most theoretically ambitious interpretations of this poem practically insist on taking as its tone an air of utmost sobriety.[34] Nevertheless, this lyric about a modernized Persephone figure works in a way similar to a set of Hogarth prints, or comic strip—by presenting a series of scenes to tell a story. Of course, all narrative sequences do this, but Dickinson's uses in "Because I could not / stop for Death – " of the dramatic gesture, compressed time, action contained within a carefully delineated structure (the stanza), and her reliance on props, montage, panning, cutting, framing, and the close-up are like the conventions of theatre and film that M. Thomas Inge locates in the techniques of the comic strip. As he rightly points out, one major difference between the strip and theatre or film is that the strip is "usually the product of one artist (or a writer and artist team) who must fulfill simultaneously the roles of scriptwriter, scene designer, director, and producer" (77). In a comic strip, the actors must be brought to life in the flat and limited space of a printed page on which there are but a few (usually four, expanded to eight on Sundays) discrete scenes drawn to tell the story. Similarly, in "Because I could not / stop for Death – " scriptwriter, scene designer, director, and producer Dickinson uses six stanzas as six vignettes to "cartoon" the ostensible subject of the speaker's relationship with death and deflate somber critical explanations that render this story without a smile.

Almost every interpreter mentions that the first stanza, or panel in the picture, presents death as a gentleman caller. Though the lyric "I" is never differentiated sexually, most readers assume the speaker is female. As criticism evolved over the past couple of decades, feminist interpretations opened new "horizons of expectations" for perusal, and clued readers to possibilities of meaning previously overlooked. For example, the trope of suitor masquerading as death himself suggests that the topic actually explored here compares marriage to a kind of death.[35]

> Because I could not
> stop for Death –
> He kindly stopped for me –
> The Carriage held but
> just Ourselves ,
> And Immortality .

How to picture the indeterminate "Immortality," as another passenger or as a disembodied quality, remains up to the reader. Is this a threesome, not a twosome? Are there three riders in the carriage—the speaker, Death, and Immortality? The second panel shows the suitor or caller driving the speaker, and who constitutes "We" is again left up to the reader:

> We slowly drove – He
> knew no haste
> And I had put away
> My labor and my leisure
> too –
> For His Civility –

The third panel may itself be a triptych, featuring stages of the day and/or of life:

> We passed the School,
> where Children strove

At Recess – in the Ring –
We passed the Fields
of Gazing Grain –
We passed the Setting Sun ˎ

The fourth panel reverses the movement described in the first three so
that the carriage appears to have stopped, and the Phoebus of the heavens
wheels by it instead of being passed by the carriage. Of course this restores
natural order, but beyond the halfway point of the lyric, description of the
speaker's clothing—stiff silks and freefloating cobwebs of gossamer—for
the first time suggests that it is Miss Havisham's suitor who has finally
come; nothing previously hinted that, like the Dickens character and her
wedding banquet, the speaker has been gathering dust.

Or rather – He passed
Us ˎ
The Dews grew quivering
and chill –
For only Gossamer, my
Gown –
My Tippet – only Tulle –

The fifth stanza reveals that the carriage stop apparent in the fourth was
in fact relative, for in this the riders pause. The house, the "Swelling of
the Ground," seems surely to be a grave, and the reader cannot help but
be surprised by this site of death and burial that, compared to the habitats
of the living, itself also appears to be growing.

We paused before a
House that seemed
A Swelling of the Ground –
The Roof was scarcely
visible –
The Cornice – in the Ground

Abstract and indeterminate, as Sharon Cameron and many others have
pointed out, the sixth and final stanza "completes" the narrative series
with its description of time as relative—centuries do not feel as long as
days—and of the easily imagined horses directed toward the hard-to-
picture dream of eternity.

Since then – 'tis Centuries –
and yet
Feels shorter than the Day
I first surmised the
Horses' Heads
Were toward Eternity –

That this poem begins and ends with humanity's ultimate dream of self-importance—Immortality and Eternity—could well be the joke central to its meaning, for Dickinson carefully surrounds the fantasy of living ever after with the dirty facts of life—dusty carriage rides, schoolyards, and farmers' fields. Many may contend that, like the Puritans and metaphysicals before her, Dickinson pulls the sublime down to the ridiculous but unavoidable facts of existence, thus imbues life on earth with its real import. On the other hand, Dickinson may have argued otherwise. Very late in her life, she wrote, "When Jesus tells us about his Father, we distrust him. When he shows us his Home, we turn away, but when he confides to us that he is 'acquainted with Grief,' we listen, for that is also an Acquaintance of our own" (L 932, 1884). Instead of sharing their faith, Dickinson may be showing the community around her, most of whom were singing "When we all get to Heaven what a day of rejoicing that will be," how selfishly selective is their belief in a system that bolsters egocentrism by assuring believers not only that their individual identities will survive death, but also that they are one of the exclusive club of the saved. Waiting for the return of Eden or Paradise, which "is always eligible" and which she "never believed . . . to be a superhuman site" (L 391, 1873), those believers may simply find themselves gathering dust. Surrounded by the faithful, Dickinson struggled with trust and doubt in Christian promises herself, but whether she believed in salvation or even in immortality is endlessly debatable.[36] Readers can select poems and letters and construct compelling arguments to prove that she did or did not. But for every declaration evincing belief, there is one like that to Elizabeth Holland:

The Fiction of "Santa Claus" always reminds me of the reply to my early question of "Who made the Bible" – "Holy Men moved by the Holy Ghost," and though I have now ceased my investigations, the Solution is insufficient –   (L 794, after Christmas 1882)

What "Because I could not / stop for Death – " will not allow is any hard and fast conclusion to be drawn about the matter. Once again, as she does in her layouts, by mixing tropes and tones Dickinson underscores the importance of refusing any singleminded response to a subject and implicitly attests to the power in continually opening possibilities by repeatedly posing questions.

The second poem examined here for its cartooning effects is the sexily suggestive "In Winter in my Room" (P 1670). While the stated subject of "Because I could not / stop for Death – " is one expected of a nineteenth-century female poet, the subject of this second selection is one not usually anticipated from her: the vivid, cartoon-like description of the erection, ejaculation, and subsequent flacidity of a phallus. The descriptions throughout ("pink lank and warm," "mottles rare," the very idea of securing a worm with a string), the serpentine shape of the poem, and the blatantly penetrating metaphors create a comic tone that general perceptions about the author have precluded our receiving.

> In Winter in my Room
> I came upon a Worm
> Pink lank and warm
> But as he was a worm
> And worms presume
> Not quite with him at home
> Secured him by a string
> To something neighboring
> And went along.
>
> A Trifle afterward
> A thing occurred
> I'd not believe it if I heard
> But state with creeping blood
> A snake with mottles rare
> Surveyed my chamber floor
> In feature as the worm before
> But ringed with power
> The very string with which
> I tied him – too
> When he was mean and new
> That string was there –
>
> I shrank – "How fair you are"!
> Propitiation's claw –
> "Afraid he hissed

Of me"?
"No cordiality" –
He fathomed me –
Then to a Rhythm *Slim*
Secreted in his Form
As Patterns swim
Projected him.

That time I flew
Both eyes his way
Lest he pursue
Nor ever ceased to run
Till in a distant Town
Towns on from mine
I set me down
This was a dream –

No Dickinson holograph of this poem exists, for it survives only in Sue's snaky transcription. Proceeding in four distinct movements, the reader is first introduced to the setting, a private room in wintertime, and the action begins with discovery of a worm. The speaker never clearly describes why, how, or even about what "worms presume," but declares that is the case and immediately opts for bondage, securing "him by a string." In this first stanza, or panel of the picture, the first six, then the last three lines rhyme or off-rhyme.

The second stanza begins misleadingly, characterizing as but a "Trifle" that which is unbelievable and makes one's blood creep with its "mottles rare" and "ringed . . . power." Such terminology suggests that the growth of the worm into a powerful snake that so stuns the speaker is in fact routine or trifling for others. At the same time, the powerful effect of the worm's metamorphosis on the speaker is underscored by the fact that just as he becomes ringed with power, the off-rhyme scheme of the stanza is interrupted by the unfitting "which," a word without a near-rhyming companion. As it becomes clear that he has outgrown the string intended to bind him, the last three lines of the stanza feature the uncharacteristically regular rhyme "too" and "new," while the last line off-rhymes with the first of the third stanza.

The third stanza or picture is not obscene, but if Dickinson had to apply for a grant from the National Endowment for the Arts, the review panel would certainly have qualms about funding a project featuring such graphic description. The description of the snake's fathoming the speaker then retracting "to a Rhythm *Slim*" seems plainly one of penetration, ejaculation in climax, and denouement. Though many have used Freud or at least pursued interpretations very similar to what I am offering here, they have repeatedly stressed Dickinson's supposed terror of male sexuality, reading the interaction of the third stanza and the flight described in the fourth in a singular way.[37] Yet just who is addressing whom in the third stanza's first line is not clear. Perhaps the snake speaks to the poem's speaker, but equally plausible, especially if the conversation gives and takes turns, is that the stanza begins with the speaker's coy exclamation to the "mean and new" snake that he is in fact "fair." Then it is the speaker, not the scary snake, whose atonement or propitiation is a compliment that hurts a little even as it "digs" in, takes hold like a claw. After the speaker expresses her or his (the gender of "I" is never differentiated) fear of "cordiality," he or she is fathomed—penetrated and understood or known—by the snake, whose projected patterns then "swim" like sperm.

The speaker takes flight in the fourth stanza to towns distant from his or her own, then "set[s] me down" that "This was a dream." But in stating the obvious—that this represents the speaker's (thus Dickinson's) fear of male sexuality—readers overlook the fact that the last stanza's first line carefully emphasizes, "That time I flew." Not every time, but *that* time. It is "cordiality," not the fathoming, which frightens the speaker. Thus, if this poem symbolizes heterosexual or homosexual (between men—the snake is male and the speaker could be either male or female) intercourse, it is not the intercourse which terrifies the speaker but the cordial relations, the coupling that would be expected to accompany sexual experience in the nineteenth century. In cartoon-like fashion Dickinson's poem suggests that readers receive its embodiment of male sexuality as a worm which grows into a snake and her speaker's ludicrous attempts to hold the slithering being with a household thread with a sense of humor.

Though critical studies like those by Peter Gay and Karen Lystra are beginning to modify general opinion, we are so accustomed to characterizing women of the period as being asexual, prudish, or frightened by sexuality, and so accustomed to characterizing Emily Dickinson as a Daisy shrinking from solar masculine power, that we are prepared to receive this poem as expression of her erotic fears. Read humorously, however, the poem becomes a pronouncement both of carnal pleasure and the reluctance of any female to become officially entangled with a male partner inside a patriarchal system designed to diminish her freedoms.[38] That the speaker is running backward, with both eyes turned toward the snake instead of toward the road, makes the account of the flight itself laughable, perhaps lampooning both the fact that most women could not avoid such official involvements and/or calling into question the official rhetoric characterizing women as too pure for sexual pleasure.

So can one argue that Emily Dickinson was a cartoonist? Certainly she is no Garry Trudeau, T. O. Sylvester, Berke Breathed, or Nicole Hollander, nor did she go public with her comic work as did her contemporaries featured in *Harper's* and *Leslie's*. Likewise, while she was alive she did not distribute her poems in the print media like Phillis Wheatley, Walt Whitman, Helen Hunt Jackson, Elizabeth Barrett Browning, Robert Frost, H.D., or any of the myriad others who wrote for conventional publication. Yet her poems share many of the features of her contemporaries who printed and distributed theirs through relatively anonymous distribution systems, and Dickinson herself is widely recognized as sharing great imaginative and expressive gifts commonly associated with both the most commercially successful versifiers and time-honored bards. Similar to those produced for the periodicals of her day and the daily newspapers of ours, her cartooning productions express a "personal social vision" that can be finally "comprehensible to a wide public" (O'Sullivan 10). Like more conventional cartoons, hers take as their subjects the public institutions of law, literature, and religion, as well as social customs of the family, courtship, and marriage.

In the layouts and sketches Higginson and Loomis Todd considered unimportant for understanding her literary project, as well as in her cartooning epistles and poems, Dickinson makes a bold philosophical statement about commitment to making and exploring opportunities for re-reading culture and society. Cultivating a sense of humor and comic vision in these cartoons, Dickinson remarks profoundly upon reading texts on pages and reading texts of social and cultural conformity writ large in macrocosmic (the church or government) and microcosmic (the family) organizations of human life.

In 1930 Robert Frost exhorted Amherst alumni and students by saying that learning to read the world, or learning to think, is learning to produce metaphor, "is just putting this and that together; it is just saying one thing in terms of another." That Dickinson knew both how to read and how to realign her world is clear from an early letter to her brother in which she appropriates "Tired of the World," an 1851 cartoon from *Punch* published in the June issue of *Harper's New Monthly Magazine*. The cartoon features a grandmother with her Holy Bible open in her lap and her granddaughter at her knee; they are before a fireplace and surrounded by dolls, balls, a dollhouse, and a floor littered with miniature furniture and an oval carton casually thrown halfway open. Beneath the sketch is the dialogue:

> *Grandmamma*—"Why, what's the matter with my Pet?"
> *Child*—"Why, Grandma, after giving the subject every consideration, I have come to the conclusion that—the World is Hollow, and my Doll is stuffed with Sawdust, so—I—should—like—if you please, to be a Nun?" (Leyda 1:201)

In a paragraph closing the letter to her brother, Dickinson echoes the cartoon: "If I had'nt been afraid that you would 'poke fun' at my feelings, I had written a *sincere* letter, but since 'the world is hollow, and Dollie is stuffed with sawdust,' I really do not think we had better expose our feelings" (L 42). As she will in her cartoon to Sue appropriating *The Old Curiosity Shop*, here Dickinson assumes Austin's conversancy with contemporary popular literature. Then she gleefully uses their mutual literacy to encode and express some of her most irreverent feelings even while she claims to hide them. The letter begins with hyperbolic descriptions of the family's missing Austin, who has just left home to teach in Boston, and is filled with mocking accounts of how their parents "take great delight in dwelling upon your character, and reviewing your many virtues" and how she found "Father in great agitation" and "Mother and Vinnie in tears, for fear that he would kill me" because she had not returned from visiting friends and neighbors until the scandalous hour of 9:00 P.M. Thus in her concluding sentences transferring onto "Dollie" her feelings of being stifled in a home that sometimes felt more like a convent, Dickinson manipulates her allusions to allow herself the freedom to express both her bit of envy for the eldest son roaming somewhat at will and her irritation at a controlling father. To underscore her jaunty mood, she concludes the paragraph, "Vinnie has commenced snoring." Choosing to respond to familial tensions with humor instead of with unalloyed resentment, Dickinson playfully masters what could have been a much more volatile situation, heartening herself beyond rigidly fixed dynamics of paternal dominance and embittered submission.

In keeping with taking responsibility for her feelings and refusing passive obedience to family forms, the creative entanglements evinced by Dickinson's cutting others' texts and by her refusal to confine herself to standardized poetic forms reflect a similar awareness of the elasticity of seemingly fixed cultural forms and readers' relationships to them. This does not show disrespect toward texts or authors, but an attitude toward reading as a generative enterprise. By sharp contrast to custom, such an attitude demystifies illusions of textual completion fostered in the literary world by the printing press and in the world at large by laws and codes of behavior. Like Shelley, Dickinson did not need intricate critical theory to be aware of textual instability, nor did she need reader-response hypotheses and principles to know that reader and text act in concert with one another to make a poem, that neither texts nor authors are static things but are to be acted upon and interacted with. Like Shelley, too, Dickinson's consciousness of the lack of fixity in moral, social, and cultural rules and regulations was not limited to the literary world. Hans Robert Jauss would say that such metaphor-making readers are travelers, open to the horizons continually unfolding before them and to the horizons continually unfolding within horizons. "I am Eve" (L 9), Dickinson claimed early in her writing career, identifying herself with a woman who may be called the first questioner since she eschewed obeisance for critical inquiry. In Judeo-Christian mythology, Eve's questions led to her and Adam's expulsion from Eden and to the first travel or exploration of new horizons. So Dickinson beckons us not to surrender to the assumption that uncertainty, new possibility, and questioning are failure and fall, but to allow that they are avenues to the investigation and search for new meaning. In these holograph productions, Emily Dickinson sportively demonstrates how carefully she thought about politics, religion, the family, sexuality, and her moment as a literary woman. Though literary conventions encourage readers and editors to speculate about what Dickinson would have done had she been forced to make choices to conform to the leveling standards of print and choose variants and shape punctuation to publish in the usual typeset way, I am persuaded that the poet saw her supposed confinement to private "publication" as liberation. To bind her to the predictable standards for choice in literary production is to overlook the choices she made, for, similar to Blake, Dickinson privatized "the roles of author, editor, illustrator, publisher, printer, and distributor," making of herself and her highly responsive audience, Sue, a literary institution unto themselves.[39] Much more so in the nineteenth century, but even today, conventional publication tends to promote authorial conservatism in order to be accepted for the print media. Thus by manufacturing her own books and cartoons and controlling her final copy, Dickinson was neither limited to poetic forms regularized by the typesetter and by the critical wisdom of her contemporaries, nor to poetic subjects deemed appropriate for lady poets. The radical nature of her poetic project is perhaps most dramatically embodied in her layouts with their sprightly delivery of social commentary. In the spirit of a cartoonist, she makes stifling cultural authorities and conventions laughable, and thereby reminds fellow challengers never to lose sight of the importance of having fun. In other words, she exhorts all readers to embrace her beatitude: "Blessed are they that play."

Chapter 4
The Humor of Excess

by Cristanne Miller

AS ANY READER of Mark Twain or Rabelais knows, humor is as apt to stem from excess, grotesquerie, unbearable qualities of humanness, or the perceived peculiarities of the human body as it is to stem from more intellectual, amiable, or obviously social sources. As well as being a teaser and a cartoonist, Dickinson is mistress of excess and of the grotesque. In poem after poem, this poet brings herself to the very point of going too far, losing control—whether of good taste, metaphorical coherence, tone, language more generally, or of narrative scene. Through the very exuberance or weirdness of her expression in such poems, Dickinson creates moments of linguistic and narrative incongruity, disruption, chaos; yet because these same poems ultimately exult in the individual's powers of endurance and the poet's power of expression—hence, the power of the human psyche and brain—they are humorous rather than merely frightening. Moreover, the poems reveal such thoughtful construction (as her frequent revisions show) that this excess seems quite consciously allowed if not always fully planned or intended.[1] Like Sappho's extraordinary and precise descriptions of just how miserable she is when rejected in love, Dickinson's descriptions of her various trials demonstrate at the least a rebellious pluckiness in always being able to distance herself from the experience far enough to case it in linguistic extravagance.

Unlike much of the humor of our culture and of her time, Dickinson's does not revolve around a butt of humor or scapegoat; she does not delight in acts of gory violence (gouging out eyeballs, and so on) performed upon specific (fictitious) individuals.[2] While, as Smith shows, she may poke fun at a stern aunt in her letters, there is no cruelty in the humor of excess in her poetry. There Dickinson rarely focuses on an "Other" to mock, and when she does the object is typically an abstraction (prayer, religion) or some person or group on at least an equal level with her (God, upper-class women) rather than a group of lesser privilege or greater marginality. Primarily, Dickinson directs excess at herself, or at the isolated female—often by means of attention to the female body. She makes herself—as cultural object or cultural "Other"—both the speaking and the perceived subject of her humor. In these poems, one sees the extreme edges of the poet's own (real or imagined) experience, the dissolution or bizarre magnification of the speaker's body, the voraciousness of her desires. This release seems to provide an opposing and corollary side to Dickinson's other kinds of female posturing—the silent, meek homebody dressed in white, or poor starving child shut out of the house; to borrow from Mary Russo, by modeling "bold affirmations of feminine performance, imposture, and masquerade," on the one hand, and "radical negation," on the other, or by modeling the contrasts of "purity and danger," Dickinson implies the boundaries of the feminine against which she rebels (213). Dickinson uses excess and grotesquerie to destabilize notions of the good woman, and of the "feminine" body.

In her poems that spill into excess, Dickinson has a less direct relation to a particular audience than in the poems discussed by either Juhasz or Smith. Here Dickinson appears to be almost an exhibitionist, flaunting the grotesquerie of her person or desire before a non-specific plural audience rather than teasing or joking with individuals, through private correspondence or the deceptive singularity of her "you." She is both more disguised in these poems and more exposed; she reveals greater extremities, more rough edges, of her psyche and perception. The arresting production of humor through excess and grotesquerie gives Dickinson's poems more a feeling of flamboyant hamming than one finds in other of her poems, or in most serious poetry.

Similarly, the relation of her humor to a particular object differs from the cases discussed in previous chapters. In her poems of excess, there is no clear ground of innocence or safety from which the speaker may mock or criticize particular aspects of the world or human nature. Instead, just as the speaker is the focus of the poem's excess, the object of the humor overlaps or becomes elided with the subject speaker such that she also becomes its object. Rather than mocking or challenging God, the publishing industry, patriarchal domestic life, or her own family, or speculating about those "Flood" subjects love, death, and immortality, here Dickinson puts her own perception and body on the line: the extremity of her revising and questioning leaves no stable position behind. These poems do contain a critique of the world (God, the family, and so on) that provokes such explosive response; the humor, however, typically points at that world indirectly, through the more immediate vehicle of deconstructing assumed aspects of the perspective and humanity of the speaker. As one might gather, then, the humor of these poems is difficult to locate because it is not pointed sharply at a particular object. Although one occasionally finds wit and open playfulness in these poems, their humor is typically more diffuse than that of other Dickinson poems.

The politics and purpose underlying such extravagance are cut from the same cloth as the politics of Dickinson's poetics generally, but they too expose themselves here in more extreme form. Humor of excess issues from the poet's profound sense of displacement, or an imagination that has been prompted by repeated experiences of alterity to fantasize a world in which nothing takes its prescribed form. Such humor finds its expression through the isolation of body parts, surreal combinations of human and non-human physical features, inappropriate responses to pain and grief, and bizarre or grotesque conceptions of common events in human life. In such poems, the disruption of norms, the critique of ordinary boundaries for life, takes the form of a general explosion of ordering assumptions about the most basic elements of life—how a body holds together, the relation of an individual to the natural world, differences between thought and action or felt and released power. The language, scenes, and patterns of these poems create disorder in the social and natural worlds—for Dickinson much the same thing as both are controlled by "Fathers" who seem to do as they please with little regard for the woman, or child, below them. So profound is the falseness of the order she perceives that she can imagine no alternative reordering or new system working from the same parts, and so demonstrates graphically and linguistically the chaos she at least occasionally would prefer to the proscribed apparent order she must live within.

As David Reynolds lavishly documents, the grotesque and excessive humor found in many of Dickinson's poems was by no means unusual in the nineteenth century. The popular frontier and, later, urban "subversive" humorists provided ample models for both the pre-surrealistic and the grotesquely comic elements of her writing. Reynolds argues, in fact, that "Dickinson's experimental style constituted . . . a transformation of progressive linguistic strategies" mostly derived from popular sensational and humorous writing: "The distinctive combination in Dickinson's major poetry of savage and comical images was characteristic of an age when the sensational and the sprightly were increasingly conjoined in the popular press" (427, 474). While T. B. Thorpe and other early nineteenth-century writers in this vein remain known primarily as minor writers of regional humor, Mark Twain, Nathaniel West, Flannery O'Connor, and other late nineteenth- and twentieth-century writers—like Dickinson—carry the excess and grotesquerie of this humor into what is more commonly regarded as literary terrain. According to Reynolds, Dickinson was the only woman of her day to make use in her own writing of the "blackly humorous images" that abounded in the popular press (429).

Despite the multiple examples of grotesque humor published both before and after Dickinson was writing her own wildly humorous verse, I find the most illuminating comparison to be an anachronistic and less obvious one—namely, a comparison of Dickinson's excessive humor with the camp productions of the twentieth century, especially as lesbian, gay, and feminist critics have analyzed the politics of camp. Dickinson's poems anticipate camp not just in their humorous extravagance, excess, and grotesque qualities, but also more specifically in their focus on the body and their strong element of performance. More profoundly, the excesses of camp and those of Dickinson's poems may share a more radical cultural subversiveness than the exuberantly amoral and violent humorous writing of the nineteenth century. Like camp, Dickinson's poems of humorous grotesquerie are simultaneously epistemological and cultural in their mocking rejection of standard ways of seeing, speaking, and being; they attempt not just to violate norms (or taste) but to open up possibilities for new ways of perceiving and being both gendered and sexual beings in a social and natural world. Dickinson would not have been familiar with the term, the concept, or the self-conscious gay culture that gave rise to camp. Nonetheless, as I argue at length later in this essay, current analyses of the politics of camp's dynamics of humor can shed considerable light on the more indirect politics of Dickinson's excessive humor.[3]

Excess can appear in many forms.[4] Those mentioned above, grotesquerie and camp, are types of excess that correspond to well-known elements of our culture and may easily be named: because their boundaries overlap, they also contribute similarly to an understanding of excess. Of these three terms, camp is the most specific and hence most useful for making certain kinds of political distinctions, but least useful as a general name for this style of Dickinson's writing. The grotesque, which is often an element of camp, may be isolated from the cultural and social associations of that more specific category and used to map out the kind of poem that concerns me here; many poems of excess contain grotesque elements and almost all poems featuring the grotesque are excessive—unless the grotesquerie has been so domesticated by the context or by popular metaphor as to make it more sentimental than surreal, as in the gothic poem "One need not be a Chamber – to be Haunted – " (670). Excess is the umbrella category for the various types of incongruity, apparent incoherence, nonconventionality, grotesquerie, and surrealism such poems display.

To begin with formal rather than cultural or associative categories, linguistic and narrative excess are the types of greatest importance to my argument. Linguistic excess occurs where Dickinson's metaphors or contrasting vocabularies create a moment of disruption or incongruity in a poem; narrative or imaginative excess occurs where the poet's scene or plot moves beyond the bounds of the literally knowable.[5] For example, excessive narrative lapses into sacrilegious cuteness in "A transport one cannot contain," where the poet imagines seeing "Holy Ghosts in Cages!" at a fair (184). In "Doubt Me! My Dim Companion!" the speaker (referring to herself in the third person) indicates through grotesque metaphors of dismemberment, or linguistic excess, her willingness to undergo trials to prove her loyalty: "Sift her, from Brow to Barefoot! / . . . Winnow her finest fondness – / But hallow just the snow / Intact, in Everlasting flake – / Oh, Caviler, for you!" (275). One sees excess in the poet's descriptions of nature: at sunset, "Mountains drip . . . Hemlocks burn . . . Steeples hand the Scarlet / Till the Ball is full – " and finally the unimaginable—"a Dome of Abyss is Bowing / Into Solitude – " (291); or, the poet hears "phraseless Melody" made by the wind "Whose fingers Comb the Sky – / Then quiver down – with tufts of Tune – " (321). Beyond relationship and nature, Dickinson imagines the possibility of almost having died as "a Face of Steel – / That suddenly looks into our's / With a metallic grin – / The Cordiality of Death – / Who drills his Welcome in – " (286). As these examples show, often linguistic and imaginative or narrative excess coincide in creating the moment of shock or epiphany in a poem.

The examples above also reveal the tendency of such poems and lines to include elements of the grotesque, particularly corporeal or sexual grotesquerie or displacement. Other poems take this tendency to a greater extreme. The speaker of 277 asks, "What if I burst the fleshly Gate – . . . What if I file this Mortal – off – "; a poem beginning "'Tis so appalling – it exhilarates – / So over Horror, it half Captivates" concludes with the poet's own conjunction of these contrasts: "Terror's free – / Gay, Ghastly, Holiday!" (281); in another poem, remembering "a Withdrawn Delight – / Affords a Bliss like Murder – / Omnipotent – Acute – " (379). Nature may be transformed with unpredictable and excruciating results. One poem laments the coming of spring: "if I could only live / Till that first Shout got by – / Not all Pianos in the Woods / Had power to mangle me – " (348). Another imagines winter as a deadly suitor: frost "Caresses – and is gone – / . . . And whatsoever Mouth he kissed – / Is as it had not been – " (391). "I tend my flowers for thee – " begins with a blooming that sounds like mass suicide: "My Fuschzia's Coral Seams /

Rip . . . / Geraniums – tint – and spot – / . . . My Cactus – splits her
Beard / To show her throat – / . . . Globe Roses – break their satin
flake – " (339). Although these lines are from poems Thomas H. Johnson
dates as early, one finds examples of excessive and macabre lines throughout her poetry.

It is a commonplace now in Dickinson criticism, as we state in Chapter 1, that this poet writes frequently of pain, death, loss, and suffering.
Many of Dickinson's poems on these subjects (including several quoted
from above) are apparently sincere expressions of empathy, fear, wonder,
or other emotions such subjects predictably evoke. Several other poems
on these ultimately serious topics, however, contain expressions, metaphors, or a narrative perspective so at odds with the expected tone that the
result is humorous.

"I like a look of Agony," for example, begins by calling attention to the
disjunction of appearance and sincerity, and by overturning good taste and
morality in its claim to like evidence of another's suffering: the speaker
likes "a look," not the experience or feeling, "of agony," and this "look"
is most often revealed by someone else's pain. She likes to appear to be
suffering, or to see signs that someone else (apparently) is. This poem
teeters between the possible multiple ironies suggested in its first statement and its more obvious sincere message.

> I like a look of Agony,
> Because I know it's true –
> Men do not sham Convulsion,
> Nor simulate, a Throe –
>
> The Eyes glaze once – and that is Death –
> Impossible to feign
> The Beads upon the Forehead
> By homely Anguish strung.   (241)

In a naïve reading, the poem states that one may trust a person's expression
of pain since no one would fake pain's effects: "Men do not sham Con-
vulsion, / Nor simulate, a Throe." In its extreme form, this claim is true:
ultimately, death is "Impossible to feign." But the poem's syntax suggests
that "Impossible to feign" refers primarily to the phrase "Beads upon the
Forehead"—or to a sign of suffering, and the appearance of suffering is in
fact feignable, as Dickinson knows, and as she implies by her word "look"
in line one. Whether the actual feeling of one in pain or the plain, apparently sincere ("homely") look of the actor, anguish provides a kind of folk-

art jewelry (sweat beads) that signifies sincerity. Anguish, then, is the ultimate mask because no one will dare to question it.

This line of reasoning implies that the poet's opening exclamation may be taken at face value: she *likes* "a look of Agony." On others, this "look" tells her that she may trust them—unless they are as crafty as she is. On herself—in one of her favorite roles, as "Queen" or "Empress" "of Calvary"—this look ensures greatest privacy in the most theatrical costume possible. "I like a look of Agony" articulates the belief which Dickinson needs as a veil to cover the artistry of her self-presentation in other poems. It contains no description or phrase that is ostensibly funny, but the note of glee in its opening claim makes one both hope and fear that at any moment the speaker's disguise, or the text's sincerity, will crack, revealing—what kind of glee? what cause for disguise?

Looking only at "I like a look of Agony" a reader might find relatively little evidence for seeing a macabre humor here; in the context of Dickinson's repeated sly mixing of suffering and humor, however, the latter becomes clearer. "I measure every Grief I meet" (561) provides another example in which Dickinson presents powerful feeling—here, grief—as artful physical disguise. In this poem, wherever the fiction of heartfelt sorrow is dislodged by the incongruity of the speaker's metaphors, an undertone of forbidden comedy gleams through.

> I measure every Grief I meet
> With narrow, probing, Eyes –
> I wonder if It weighs like Mine –
> Or has an Easier size.
>
> I wonder if They bore it long –
> Or did it just begin –
> I could not tell the Date of Mine –
> It feels so old a pain –
>
> I wonder if it hurts to live –
> And if They have to try –
> And whether – could They choose between –
> It would not be – to die –
>
> I note that Some – gone patient long –
> At length, renew their smile –
> An imitation of a Light
> That has so little Oil –

I wonder if when Years have piled –
Some Thousands – on the Harm –
That hurt them early – such a lapse
Could give them any Balm –

Or would they go on aching still
Through Centuries of Nerve –
Enlightened to a larger Pain –
In Contrast with the Love –

The Grieved – are many – I am told –
There is the various Cause –
Death – is but one – and comes but once –
And only nails the eyes –

There's Grief of Want – and Grief of Cold –
A sort they call "Despair" –
There's Banishment from native Eyes –
In sight of Native Air –

And though I may not guess the kind –
Correctly – yet to me
A piercing Comfort it affords
In passing Calvary –

To note the fashions – of the Cross –
And how they're mostly worn –
Still fascinated to presume
That Some – are like My Own –   (561)

Here the speaker describes herself as a fashion-monitor, critically observing the various garbs of grief the way a top model would analyze designer clothing: how long will the cloth wear, how was the garment constructed, is it as spectacular as mine?[6] The poem's middle stanzas enumerate the speaker's speculations about "the fashions" of grief passing before her "probing, Eyes" in a panorama analogous to life itself. Rather than empathizing with fellow sufferers, the poem's narrator speculates about their endurance and impersonally categorizes their suffering ("There's Grief of Want – and Grief of Cold . . ."). Although she receives "piercing Comfort" from her observations, she is playing a game: to "guess . . . Correctly" what has produced each of grief's multiple fashions. "Death"—although the ultimate grief—shows lack of imagination and endurance: it "comes but once – / And only nails the eyes – ," providing a look of little interest in comparison with the panoply of more imaginative and actively suffering fashions. Again calling into question the naïve claim that one cannot feign the effects of grief, Dickinson here suggests that people compete in exhibiting their agonies (is yours "Easier" than hers?). She seems to invite people to flaunt their wounds, join the show. The whole metaphor of fashion suggests that one chooses and changes what one exhibits, that feeling may be taken off and put on; it invites the reader to imagine this narrator looking into her emotional mirror each morning to check how her "Grief" looks today.

Humor of excess has several topics and modes besides that represented in the two poems above. "These are the Nights that Beetles love – ," for example, is a more accessibly comic poem, in part because it contains lines as conventionally sentimental as one can find anywhere in Dickinson's verse. Yet descriptive extravagance and fragmental syntax—along with a few lines of speculative reasoning utterly divorced from sentimentality—move the poem out of the conventional and into the realm of excess.

> These are the Nights that Beetles love –
> From Eminence remote
> Drives ponderous perpendicular
> His figure intimate
> The terror of the Children
> The merriment of men
> Depositing his Thunder
> He hoists abroad again –
> A Bomb upon the Ceiling
> Is an improving thing –
> It keeps the nerves progressive
> Conjecture flourishing –
> Too dear the Summer evening
> Without discreet alarm –
> Supplied by Entomology
> With it's remaining charm   (1128)

The beetle is both sublime and ridiculous: "he" emerges from on high and terrifies children, but adults ("men") laugh at his maneuvers. This insect stands, however, for the possibility of terror in a way that is instructive: "A Bomb upon the Ceiling" "improv[es]" one's nervous condition—suggesting that danger lies not in becoming too excited or overwrought but rather in becoming too dull, too unimaginative, complacent. For "progressive" nerves, Dickinson advises, put yourself in a position of potential danger. For full, imaginative alertness, one requires at least "discreet alarm[s]." As the last lines of the poem imply, there is an analogy between "merriment" that has its roots in "terror," a lively or "flourishing" imagination, and a full appreciation of life. Summer would be "Too dear" without the beetle's threatened "Thunder" because it is the beetle that makes one know oneself firmly in life—in the realm of terror and laughter—rather than in some partial heaven. Yet it is precisely the beetle's "ponderous perpendicular" descent that makes the hilarity of the evening, or that provides the occasion for the memory focusing the speaker's love of life. Although many of Dickinson's poems of grotesquerie take real suffering or terror as the theme against which their humor plays, this poem is not unusual in its affirmative, more obviously comic tone and conclusion.

E. B. White writes that "Humor can be dissected, as a frog can, but the thing dies in the process and the innards are discouraging to any but the pure scientific mind."[7] This is no doubt true, but when the humor of something is not apparently funny, as the kind of humor I am discussing generally is not, dissection seems the only way to make its workings clear. Examining the differences in tone between "These are the Nights that Beetles love," and "I like a look of Agony" and "I measure every Grief I meet," helps to explain the peculiar nature of the humor in the two poems first discussed. Although "These are the Nights" contains elements that take it out of the world of ordinary knowledge or behavior, these elements are carefully circumscribed—both textually in the poem and epistemologically. The quatrain about the "Bomb upon the Ceiling" is preceded and followed by lines explicitly detailing the harmlessness of the situation the speaker is in, or remembers: the "Bomb" is in fact just a "Beetle," an object of "merriment" for all but "Children." Equally important in limiting the effect of these lines' disruption, the speaker presents the threat of the "Bomb" in the form of a rule: it is good for one's health to have a "Bomb"; one ought to encourage disruption. Such a dictatorial statement, while shocking in its actual content, cannot by definition be radical; its form and frame mediate the shock. If the doctor prescribes a bomb on the ceiling along with an apple a day, the bomb cannot be truly disruptive. One must simply learn how to see the proper place of this kind of disorder—learn to respond with adult "merriment" rather than with childish "terror." As I suggest by my use of terms above, one might argue that this is more what Umberto Eco would call a "comic" than a "humorous" poem: it appears to move beyond the laws of our presuppositions, but may not. It leans toward an apparent violation but real affirmation of the status quo.

And yet, this poem never altogether escapes the disruptive edge of its suggested violence. The poem's metonymy, like all metaphor, works in two directions. By comparing the bomb to a beetle, one makes the bomb harmless; by comparing the beetle to a bomb, however, one suggests that the children may be right to respond with terror—there may be more real danger in the small events of every day than adult wisdom would acknowledge. Dickinson introduces the bomb in prescriptive form, thereby suggesting that it is good for us, but such a prescription in real life would make us suspect the doctor of being a maniac, more akin to "Dr. Strangelove" than to the family physician. How harmless, then, is the speaker's intent? Similarly, the opening description of the beetle ("From Eminence remote / Drives ponderous perpendicular / His figure intimate")—pompous in its polysyllabic latinate density and disruptive in relation to the surrounding syntax—opens a gap in one's understanding of the creature described that is never adequately filled by the harmlessness of its name ("Beetle") and of the adults' response to its presence. There is something spooky and elevated as well as something ridiculous about this beetle.

In contrast, "I like a look" and "I measure every Grief" contain no elements of overt comedy. Nothing in either poem declares it harmless; nothing suggests that "merriment" is the appropriate audience response. By the same token, there is no statement of a rule to domesticate the pain and suffering of each speaker's concern. Humor appears only through the details of the text, in the mode of expression, not at all in the narrative scene or dominant fiction of the speaker's stance. Read as serious statements, the poems might be seen to reveal some neurosis on the part of a speaker who would linger at such length and with pride on her suffering, but they do not seem excessive. Only when they are read as humorous, or parodic, monologues, does the excess become apparent: it is not excessive to imagine suffering, only to imagine one who feigns it to gain an improvement on her everyday wardrobe, or who surveys it competitively, looking for a manifestation of it she would admire. And although the poems themselves direct us to such a reading through their language ("a look," "beads," "fashions") only the reader with the "rare Ear" (as Juhasz puts it) will read Dickinson's words literally as well as figuratively, thereby allowing them the full range of their meaning.

More importantly, after noting the humorous potential of these poems, one is forever caught between their possibilities for interpretation, forever disrupted, forced to decide whether or not to distrust even what seems to be most sincere. This is the effect of the humor of excess in Dickinson's poetry: it disrupts boundaries of knowing, of presupposed certainty, without substituting any new rules or certainties in their place. As Eco writes of all humor, "it undermines the law" (8).

In an essay on situation comedy of the 1950s, Patricia Mellencamp similarly outlines the difference the reader's perspective will make in his or her analysis of comedy. Quoting Jean Beaudrillard to illuminate the dynamics of *The George Burns and Gracie Allen Show*, Mellencamp writes:

> "The witticism, which is a transgressive reversal of discourse, does not act on the basis of another code as such; it works through the instantaneous deconstruction of the dominant discursive code. It volatizes the category of the code, and that of the message." The "dominant discursive code" of patriarchy tried, through benevolent George, to contain Gracie's volatization, her literal deconstruction of speech, and her tall tales of family. Whether or not the system won can be answered either way, depending on where the analyst is politically sitting—with George in his den, or in the kitchen with the women. (94)

Like Gracie, Dickinson appears to be in control of her irrationality or linguistic incongruity (and thus to "win" as poet against the system that would confine her to "natural" or sincere expression?) only if the reader is willing to imagine this possibility—to sit with her, as it were, rather than with more traditional poets.

Within the realm of response that recognizes humor, Mellencamp further distinguishes between a reader's response that identifies with the actor (or speaker) and a response that maintains its distance. Using Freud, she distinguishes humor from comedy more loosely than Eco but along similar lines:

> humorous pleasure for Freud comes from "an economy in expenditure upon feeling" rather than from the lifting of inhibitions that is the source of pleasure in jokes . . . Unlike the supposedly "liberating" function of jokes, humorous pleasure "saves" feeling because the reality of the situation is too painful. As Lucy poignantly declared to Ethel, "It's not funny, Ethel. It's tragic." Or as Freud states, "the situ-

ation is dominated by the emotion that is to be avoided, which is of an unpleasurable character." (93)

Continuing with this line of thought, Mellencamp uses Freud's categories to explain the different reactions of male and female spectators to the *I Love Lucy* show and the failure of most audiences and critics to notice the feminist strain of the comedy.

> Humor for Lucy was " a means of obtaining pleasure in spite of the distressing affects that interfere[d] with it." It acted precisely "as a substitute" for these affects. Humor was "a substitute" produced "at the cost of anger instead of getting angry." As Freud observes, "the person who is the victim of the injury, pain . . . might obtain *humourous* pleasure, while the unconcerned person laughs from *comic* pleasure." Perhaps in relation to husband and wife sketches, and audiences, the sexes split right down the middle, alternating comic with humorous pleasure depending on one's view of who the victim is . . . the response of the spectator is split between comic and humorous pleasure, between denial of emotion by humor and the sheer pleasure of laughter provided by the comic of movement and situation of Lucy's performances. (92, 93, 94)[8]

In Dickinson's poetry of excess, there is little or no opportunity for "sheer pleasure" because the humor never fully "substitutes" for the emotion it would cover: grief, anger, fear, and other feelings continue to show through. Purely pleasurable or comic response to these poems is also denied because there is no way for the reader both to maintain distance and to perceive humor or comedy at all. In short, and to repeat, these are not *funny* poems. To hear humor in them, one must read Dickinson's words literally, allowing the excess of her metaphors or narratives full play, and at the same time one must recognize the subversive or ironic element present in creating that excess. Such recognition stems, typically, from empathy or concern, thus blocking a response of unalloyed or distanced pleasure. In reading these poems, the grimace is never far behind the guffaw or grin.

"We dream – it is good we are dreaming – " (531) provides a particularly obvious example of shifting boundaries of tonality and response because it questions whether anyone may survive the pain of human life while "awake." Although the primary metaphor of the poem puns on the intersection of dramatic and childish "play," there is no ostensible humor or performance in this poem, an absence that makes Dickinson's pun especially chilling.

> We dream – it is good we are dreaming –
> It would hurt us – were we awake –
> But since it is playing – kill us,
> And we are playing – shriek –
>
> What harm? Men die – externally –
> It is a truth – of Blood –
> But we – are dying in Drama –
> And Drama – is never dead –
>
> Cautious – We jar each other –
> And either – open the eyes –
> Lest the Phantasm – prove the Mistake –
> And the livid Surprise
>
> Cool us to Shafts of Granite –
> With just an Age – and Name –
> And perhaps a phrase in Egyptian –
> It's prudenter – to dream –   (531)

Unlike "I like a look of Agony" and "I measure every Grief," here is a poem about terrible suffering that pretends to be lighthearted. "What harm?" if we "die" daily in the game of "shriek," it asks, since this is only the internal pain of "Drama." And yet were we to test our assumption that our present suffering occurs only in a dream (and therefore doesn't really "hurt us"), "the Phantasm" might "prove the Mistake," and we might lose the small protection we have from conscious suffering. To face our present life with full consciousness in the constant threat of death would be to die, Dickinson implies—anticipating Freud's notion of substitution or denial of pain in humor. Such "livid Surprise" would "Cool us to Shafts of Granite" or tombstones, complete with Egyptian inscription. In the poem's strongest moment of humor, Dickinson suggests that we would become monuments of the once living for future "players" and graveyard tourists to puzzle over; consciousness would ironically transform us into artifacts rather than making us actors in, or even the audience to, our own play.

The vocabulary of this poem suggests that moment in children's play where they become too wound up and their silliness metamorphoses into the "shriek" of anger or tears—that is, where the silliness ceases to be fun(ny). Like a child's game gone awry, the poem provides no reassuring rule or explanation. As in the first two poems I discuss, and despite the vocabulary of play, no narrative commentary or event returns this poem's ghoulishness to the level of the playful; some creator greater than ourself—"it," perhaps God—teases us in what remains a terrible game. Humor here occurs in the irony of the speaker's conundrum: the play of "shriek" cannot "hurt us" as long as we are only dreaming, but if we try to reassure each other of even this fact through actual contact, we run the risk of discovering that the pain does hurt—either because we aren't dreaming, or because we may wake each other up. In dreams, as in the poem, the price of remaining in a state of only questionable pain, of continuing to believe we are just playing a game, is isolation. On the other hand, the speaker's flippant tone and her casual refusal to be cowed by actual death lend a more obvious humor to the poem. The speaker dismisses death as "external," merely "a truth – of Blood – ." With this dismissal, she seems to boast that "dying in Drama" involves greater suffering than actual death, while at the same time she claims that drama protects us from "hurt." Moreover, in what seems the voice of a child savant, the speaker implies that we choose our earthly condition—"It's prudenter – to dream – " she tells us, as if advising us not even to consider other options for life.

The bleakness of what I am calling humor in these poems of Dickinson's seems less odd when examined in the light of analyses of humor that stress the serious or painful underpinning of this phenomenon rather than the humor born of satisfaction and happiness. In the *Handbook of Humor Research*, Joel Goodman writes that "Humor is laughter made from pain" (12). As we quote in the introduction, Nancy Walker writes that "Even when, as is frequently the case, [women's humor] points to the myriad absurdities that women have been forced to endure in this culture, it carries with it not the lighthearted feeling that is the privilege of the powerful, but instead a subtext of anguish and frustration" (*A Very Serious Thing* xii). In his chronological exploration of American humorous writing, Neil Schmitz argues that although "true humor" is essentially "amiable" and forgiving, humor generally requires pain, or suffering, or danger as its fundamental subject; without the backdrop or material of harsh seriousness, there is no place for the questionings and reexaminings of humor (11, 127–128). Similarly, although Schmitz distinguishes humor from irony as a less negative and therefore more fully adequate, balanced, or rounded perspective on the world, he claims that "humor contains a much deeper scepticism than irony" (13). Schmitz claims Twain as the first American humorist along the lines he describes; nonetheless, his descriptions fit Dickinson's verse very closely. Her humor of excess typically works from a serious or painful situation, at the same time that her ability to articulate aspects of the situation in a personal, often colloquial, idiosyncratic way gives the poem an ultimately affirmative basis.

As indicated in the examples above, the grotesque plays a major role in Dickinson's poems of excess and, as in all grotesquerie, the human body provides Dickinson's primary subject in this mode. In any context, the body would be a culturally loaded subject for a Victorian woman, much more in the context of excess, grotesquerie, and humor. Eco, Schmitz, and others argue that humor is necessarily disruptive of authority; if feminist humor in particular places itself in antagonistic relation to the norms of niceness and of gentility (socially denominated as female), then the macabre is a logical field for feminist humorous play—again, as seen in Lucille Ball's comically grotesque distortions of housewifery and femininity. Certainly Juhasz sees the extremes of Dickinson's (socially sanctioned) teasing as leaning in the direction of excess. On the other hand, Walker and others describe the social constraints on women not to be publicly funny because the requirements of humor contradict those of proper womanhood, and one who is humorous in the modes of grotesquerie or excess steps even further outside these proper boundaries.[9]

Moreover, in the nineteenth century, a white, middle-class woman's body was seen as the primary locus and source of her all-encompassing gender identification, yet her body was also taboo as a subject for feminine exploration or discussion. Therefore to write of the female body in poems of humorous excess was to depart just about as far as possible from all norms of propriety and "good" girl or womanhood. In her most radical poems of humorous excess, Dickinson not only writes of but literally deconstructs the female body, littering pieces of it around the landscape of her mind.[10] Although her references are often not sexual and for that reason not overtly immoral by her community's standards, their very physicality takes them outside the realm of proper writing for a woman. For this reason, such poems on the body constitute an important part of Dickinson's resistance to dominant constructions of gender, and point to the gender politics that may underlie even those poems with no apparent stake in gender roles or the feminine. Other poems appear, or begin as, ungendered, but imply that the body under discussion is feminine in its positionality if not outright female.

For example, "A still – Volcano – Life – " begins by making disruptive thoughts or feelings of "Life" concrete through the metaphor of a (nongendered) volcano.

A still – Volcano – Life –
That flickered in the night –
When it was dark enough to do
Without erasing sight –

A quiet – Earthquake Style –
Too subtle to suspect
By natures this side Naples . . .

The poem's first two stanzas emphasize the secrecy of such a life. At the end of the second stanza, however, Dickinson moves out from the abstract soul to the physical (and in this case implicitly gendered) body to give more intimate and immediate impact to her metaphor:

The North cannot detect

The Solemn – Torrid – Symbol –
The lips that never lie –
Whose hissing Corals part – and shut –
And Cities – ooze away –   (601)

The multiple suggestive aspects of female sexuality in the final stanza's images (the speaker's undetected, clearly non-phallic, metonymic ability to "ooze"; the coral lips which might belong either to the mouth or to the more frighteningly "quiet" vagina; and perhaps even the volcanic heaving bosom) point to the centrality of the body in imagining this Life's eruption.

As with all of Dickinson's metaphors of grotesquerie, this stanza offers two surreal pictures. In the first, a speaker's "hissing Corals" part to release lava-like words, expressions, or fluid so destructive that "Cities" are destroyed. One of the more chilling aspects of this image lies in the lack of anger or intention in the volcano's action: whether the speaker utters curses or merely parts her lips in a smile, the result is equally destructive. At the same time, the metaphor depicts a volcanic mountain with the "lips" of a siren, sensuously "hissing," "part[ing]" and "shut[ting]" as it slowly releases its molten rock. In either case, the body disappears except for the magnified and red lips, which give immediate and frighteningly controlled release to the "Volcano – Life" within. In a grotesque metonymy, a woman becomes a mouth—or that other dangerous and lipped

female orifice—spewing violent destruction. Here there is no obvious humanity to which a victim of the "hissing Corals" might appeal.

Speech is both deadly and sexual in another poem that calls attention to
the body, although this time the imagined body appears as the non-
gendered object or victim of a woman's speech rather than as the words'
source.

> She dealt her pretty words like Blades –
> How glittering they shone –
> And every One unbared a Nerve
> Or wantoned with a Bone –
>
> She never deemed – she hurt –
> That – is not Steel's Affair –
> A vulgar grimace in the Flesh –
> How ill the Creatures bear –
>
> To Ache is human – not polite –
> The Film upon the eye
> Mortality's old Custom –
> Just locking up – to Die.   (479)

The subject of this poem resembles both a skilled surgeon and a sword-
bearing Circe. Her "pretty"—that is, apparently harmless—words pierce
beneath the skin, then play there: "every One" "wanton[ing] with a
Bone – ." Unlike the volcanic speaker of "hissing Corals," who seems
utterly deliberate in the devastation she releases, this speaker "never
deemed – she hurt – / That – is not Steel's Affair – "; like a Pedro
Almódovar film's protagonist, she is careless of others' pain in a suggestively sexual way.[11] She teases, "wanton[s]" with her victims, enticing them
with "glittering" words into an "Affair" inevitably damaging to these
"Creatures" because her very nature is "Steel." Here Dickinson imagines
utmost, irresponsible sexual and violent power in phallic and female form.
As this paradox suggests, by assuming the prerogatives of male power, the
speaker becomes not only dangerous but unwomanly—to the extent that
womanhood is defined by the practice of empathy, or niceness. This
speaker is playful, casual, unconcerned while her listeners lie naked ("unbared") beneath her penetrating verbal "Blades."

The poem ends with a broad statement about human capacity to bear
pain and the propriety of revealing it, leaving the speaker or source of pain
behind. Whatever has caused our suffering, we are schooled not to show

it at the same time that such experience is a condition of our humanness—"To Ache is human – not polite – ." In this taboo against revelation or articulated experience, pain is like sex in yet another way: it is shameful, embarrassing to describe one's experience of it. Flesh involuntarily "grimace[s]" but the victim should not speak when words "wanton" with or "unbare" vital parts. The body is both a thing to be stripped even beneath the skin, and a mere extension of the grimacing face, its most readable feature.

"She dealt her pretty words" presents a unique variant on Dickinson's "rape" poems. Here, as in "He fumbles at your Soul" (315) or "The Soul has Bandaged moments – " (512), power is sexual. The attacking or caressing or wantoning figure enjoys apparently complete control over his or her apparently helpless victim. The difference of gender in this poem, however, makes it distinct. Where the aggressor is female, the relationship between the parties remains impersonal: "she" does not seem to care about the effects of her words, and the narrator tells us that the pain of receiving them is simply part of "Mortality's old Custom" anyway. The plural and nonhuman designation of her victims as "Creatures" contributes to the impression that their pain is a matter of indifference to her. In the other poems, the sexuality is more explicit and more personal, and the power is somewhat more equally distributed: one might argue that the female victims of "He fumbles" or "The Soul has Bandaged moments" either respond to or repeatedly escape from their tormenters.[12] In "She dealt," however, the only identified female is the speaker with her words of "Steel"—a figure who, while gendered, remains bodiless in distinct contrast to the exposed parts—Nerve, Bone, Flesh—of her ungendered listeners.

As in "I measure every Grief" and "We dream," humor in these poems of vivisection lies in discrepancies between the poems' profoundly serious subjects (the explosive power of repressed internal rebellion, and the incisive power of artfully wielded language) and the extremes of their metaphors or apparent casualness of tone. If one regarded the poems' metaphors as merely decorative, ornamental, one might dismiss their extremity and hence feel no shock. To follow their implications as far as Dickinson herself takes them, however—that is, to follow her in imaginatively literalizing the metaphors, giving them their full resonance—necessarily brings one to a limbo of contradictory responses. A human volcano, with lips prominent and sensual, whose expressions make "Cities – ooze away" evokes horror, disbelief, but also amusement at the incongruity of the speaker's self-aggrandizing fantasy: the speaker implies that she might at any time choose to open her coral lips and release destruction, that beneath her white dress lies volcanic fury. Similarly, "She dealt her pretty words" depicts, at the ornamental level, a charming woman with a sharp tongue—a stock figure in fiction. Read literally, however, this charming tease becomes a phallically empowered, knife-breathing freak, whose every wanton nuance or inflection performs surgery on one's most intimate internal parts. Here, also, the light, even genteel, tone of words like "pretty," "unbared," "glittering," "ill," and "polite," as well as the use of colloquialisms making the speaker's voice sound ordinary, unconcerned (for example, "Mortality's old Custom – / Just locking up – to Die"), contradicts the grotesqueries of the metaphor itself. There is no stable ground here: the pain caused by "words like Blades" is real, yet it is trivialized, as is human ability to bear it. The speaker is having fun—"how ill" you take a joke, she seems to say.

The conjunction of corporeality, underlying sexuality, and a critique of gender conventions is particularly obvious in these two poems, where feminine speakers become terribly powerful without appearing violent; they "merely" speak. Dickinson may also be parodying nineteenth-century gender conventions in other poems of excess less obviously linked to gender— for example, by exaggerating the stereotyped female concern with fashion and grief in "I like a look of Agony" and "I measure every Grief." Fashion has long been seen as a female domain, and sorrow is one of the dominant themes of women's popular poetry in the nineteenth century; by marking fashions of grief, Dickinson may be trebly mocking both the gendered concerns (fashion and grief) that are her subjects and popular poetry—at the same time that she (re)produces all three. In contrast, "We dream," contains no gendered bodies or associations; its corporeality is neutral. All people risk the "livid Surprise" of "Cool[ing] . . . to Shafts of Granite," or inhuman transformation in death. This poem displays a body in pain ("we are playing – shriek"), but not one that is identifiably female or feminine. Gender enters in here as a concern only through our knowledge of the gender of the author and of modes of propriety for nineteenth-century middle- and upper-class women. To repeat, in a society where it was impolite to speak of a chicken's "breast" or a table's "leg," to deal with the body at all in deliberately corporeal ways smacked of the taboo and hence of rebellion against gender codes.

The confluence between humor, sexuality, and pain in these poems— while at first shocking—makes a kind of logical sense. First, all are elements outside of normal control: one does not normally choose the precise moment and type of pain one experiences, or choose to laugh, or choose one's particular sensation of sexual arousal or orgasm. As Maurice Charney more bluntly puts it in speaking of sex and humor: "laughter, like orgasm, is an involuntary muscle spasm" (*Handbook* 33). To the extent that all three phenomena entail moments outside logical control and without limitable barriers, all are basic to an understanding of excess—or excess is a crucial element of each. Similarly, one might say that each of these basic human experiences partakes of, or leads one into, chaos, the realm of utter freedom but also utter fright if one doubts one's ability to return to the normalcy of reason and control. As the articulation of moments or experiences of chaos, poems of excess would logically rebel against conventions of all sorts, not just gender.

There may be a further link between Dickinson's poems of excess and sexuality. I suggested earlier that pain is a taboo subject in polite company and Walker argues that humor (especially in its sharper or bleaker forms) is taboo for women in public or mixed-sex company. Dickinson may feel a thrill in the repeated performance or exhibition of these taboos that resembles the sexual, or that stimulates her to link the three elements. Karl Keller argues quite specifically that Dickinson seeks "to put poetry to the service of prolonging one's sexual thrills, one's orgasms" (*Kangaroo* 266–267, 273). In all the heightened sensation of her verse, Keller sees manipulative sexual arousal, and he calls the poet a "prig-tease," enticing and distancing her reader (274). According to Keller, Dickinson, like Whitman, develops "a literary representation of the heroism of the anarchic, autonomous personality." Thus he reads her "extravagance of style as a disguise of the writer" and her sexual posing as a kind of camp.[13]

Dickinson would not, in her time, have had a basis for thinking of herself in the politicized and self-conscious terms of sexual preference, but she clearly saw herself as deviant from the norms of domestic womanhood and of respected poets in her time, and she knew that her poems departed from norms for poetry. Yet at the same time, by her late twenties, Dickinson had worked out a way of passing for at least a normal eccentric of her time. By exaggerating the characteristics of stereotyped womanhood (modesty, domesticity, devotion to one's parents, fear of and disdain for the public world, child-like behavior and perceptions), the poet created a combined mask and wall behind which she could write her intensely aggressive, astute, disruptive poems. One might almost say that to all but her most intimate friends (perhaps only Sue and immediate family members), Dickinson "passed" as a conventionally feminine woman rather than appearing in her various chosen roles: child-woman, mischievous boy, responsible (female) housekeeper, and alternately queen-like or equally powerful but non-gendered poet. This more generalized notion of deviance from cultural and aesthetic norms may lie at the root of her excessive, sometimes grotesque, imagination and humor. Perhaps as a way of calling all normative categorizing into question, Dickinson collapses the boundaries of the trivial, the aesthetic, the hideous, the humorous, and the profound, asserting that in her independent woman's life there are few differences among them.

The outrageousness of camp humor stems both from frustrated powerlessness to change a world that is oppressively masculine, straight, decorous, taboo-ridden, and serious, and from the simultaneous knowledge of the tenuousness and fragility of those boundaries and one's own role in maintaining them. Dickinson's list of frustrations would read differently: the world is narrowmindedly religious, oppressively patriarchal, categorical in its conceptions of a woman's proper sphere and fruitful life, and in conceiving proper objects and channels for feeling; yet the lists are similar enough and Dickinson is conscious enough of the source of these frustrations to give the analogy force. Dickinson even articulates her simultaneous consciousness of restriction or imprisonment and of the prison's fragility in a poem unintentionally punning on what becomes a primary metaphor for homosexual life: one may escape the restrictions of the "Closet"—for Dickinson, a closet of conventional expectations or what she calls "Prose"—simply by willing or laughing them away:

> They shut me up in Prose –
> As when a little Girl
> They put me in the Closet –
> Because they liked me "still" –
>
> Still! Could themself have peeped –
> And seen my Brain – go round –
> They might as wise have lodged a Bird
> For Treason – in the Pound –
>
> Himself has but to will
> And easy as a Star
> Abolish his – Captivity –
> And laugh – No more have I –   (613)

Whatever one's "Treason," the rebel "has but to will . . . And laugh" to "Abolish his – Captivity." In camp humor, laughter is the sign of exactly this kind of willed rejection of one world—a "Closet"—for the creation of an as yet undefined other.

Keller identifies as camp a teasing behavior much like what Juhasz describes in Chapter 2; I see Dickinson's camp more clearly in her poems' humorously distorted corporeality and grotesque or socially isolated sexuality. Definitions of camp allow for both possibilities.[14] According to Susan Sontag, who divorces camp from its explicitly political context to discuss it primarily as style, camp is extravagant, excessive, exaggerated, passionate, irrepressible, and yet stylized, concerned with artifice; it understands all aspects of being as role-play. It is detached, comic, anti-serious yet with a "new, more complex relation to 'the serious.' One can be serious about the frivolous, frivolous about the serious" (288). Importantly, camp does not reverse old polarities; rather—as Eco says of humor—it introduces a different set of standards. As an example, Sontag turns to twentieth-century visual art—"whose goal is not that of creating harmonies but of overstraining the medium and introducing more and more violent, and irresolvable, subject matter. . . . Something is good not because it is achieved, but because another kind of truth about the human situation, another experience of what it is to be human—in short, another valid sensibility—is being revealed" (287).

In *Mother Camp*, Esther Newton gives a simpler and consciously political definition: camp is "homosexual humor and taste," a strategy for survival in the gay world that concerns itself with "a philosophy of transformations and incongruity" (3, 104).[15] Analogous to *soul* in the black community, camp inheres "not in any act or thing but in *a relationship between* things, people, and activities or qualities, and homosexuality . . . in the tension between [a] person or thing and the context or association" (105, 107).[16] Despite her definition of camp as explicitly homosexual, Newton argues that the incongruous juxtapositions of camp may involve any number of differences besides those of gender and sex—for example, high and low status, sacred and profane functions or symbols, or cheap and expensive goods (107). Similarly, one may be in "drag" without assuming the appearance of the "opposite" gender; Greta Garbo, for example, is in "high camp" feminine drag in movies like *Mata Hari*, where she as self-consciously and deceptively assumes the exaggerated poses of femininity as any male impersonator. The key to drag, as to camp, is self-conscious (deviant) manipulation of a role or of roles generally. Humor is the weapon of camp (111).[17]

While neither Sontag's nor Newton's description of camp exactly fits Dickinson's work, both contribute elements that are useful for understanding the dynamics of her poems of excessive humor and corporeal or sexual displacement.[18] Sontag's insight that camp validates "another" (or we might say: an "other") sensibility and Newton's location of camp in "the tension between" an event, claim, or object and its whole sociological and historical context are particularly helpful in reading these poems.

Equally helpful is Andrew Ross' formulation that early camp (and here he means pre-1969) provided a "way of imaginatively expressing its common conquest of everyday oppression" (17). Think, for example, of Dickinson's "still – Volcano – Life," with its red hot lips "Whose hissing Corals part – and shut" in what might be as intimate as a kiss or as casual as a "hello" (601). This poem suggests a sensibility that values a sexually female power wholly alien to (or in tension with) notions of femininity in a staid New England community. Another poem, "It would have starved a Gnat – / To live so small as I," features a speaker who lives grotesquely, with "Food's necessity // Upon me – like a Claw," and fantasizes about "the Art . . . To gad my little Being out" (612), thereby calling attention to the body in a reversal of camp's ordinary gesture—making the body disappear rather than making it hyper-present. One might argue that Dickinson's several poems about not eating constitute an inverse display: "see how small I am, how little I need." Taken as serious claims of anorexic or affection-starved fantasy, the poems reveal neurosis, not humor. Read, however, as another in a variety of strategies through which Dickinson exhibits an excessively present or absent body as a way of proclaiming herself to be outside the prescribed boundaries of conventional womanhood, these poems have a clear *camp* side. They flaunt their difference just as the drag-queen does hers/his.[19]

In another poem, Dickinson describes the aftermath of some unnamed catastrophe by contrasting the erratic motion of her past life with present "paralysis":

I've dropped my Brain – My Soul is numb –
The Veins that used to run
Stop palsied – 'tis Paralysis
Done perfecter on stone.

Vitality is Carved and cool.
My nerve in Marble lies –
A Breathing Woman
Yesterday – Endowed with Paradise.

Now her veins are palsied, her nerve lies in marble; but "Yesterday,"

Not dumb – I had a sort that moved –
A Sense that smote and stirred –
Instincts for Dance – a caper part –
An Aptitude for Bird –

Who wrought Carrara in me
And chiselled all my tune
Were it a Witchcraft – were it Death –
I've still a chance to strain

To Being, somewhere – Motion – Breath –
Though Centuries beyond,
And every limit a Decade –
I'll shiver, satisfied.   (1046)

Before, a jumble of disjointed fragments (a sort, Sense, Instincts, part, Aptitude), she is now coolly unified in stone, and wondering—with a sly pun on materiality and theft—"Who . . . chiselled all my tune." Tension here lies in the unnaturalness of both descriptions of living; this speaker has no humanly recognizable features in either version of her life. Her body is the stage or canvas for her exaggerated acting out of feeling, and while her previous state is preferable to paralysis, both are grotesque displays of what cannot ordinarily be seen. At the same time, Dickinson adds a humorous edge to this disruption with her full rhyme of the serious "Sense that . . . stirred" with the ridiculous "Aptitude for Bird" and her pun on "chiselled"—both poetic effects revealing craft rather than loss of control.

A poem taking a different tack towards embodiment is the more obviously comic and campy "The Lightning is a yellow Fork," in which Dickinson gives ridiculously physical form to God.

The Lightning is a yellow Fork
From Tables in the sky
By inadvertent fingers dropt
The awful Cutlery

Of mansions never quite disclosed
And never quite concealed
The Apparatus of the Dark
To ignorance revealed.   (1173)

Here Dickinson overturns the Calvinist symbology still prevalent in early nineteenth-century revivalism that imagines God wielding lightning bolts as instruments of punishment aimed at individual sinners to imagine instead a gluttonous deity with bad table manners inadvertently stabbing things below with his "dropt" fork. Utterly unspiritual, the deity appears as "fingers" and, metonymically, as "Apparatus"—a word pertaining either to the dropped cutlery or to the mechanism behind it. God is not omnipotent, omnipresent, vengeful; he is a clumsy rube at dinner on a "Dark" stage. Moreover, the "Apparatus" controlling the stage-curtain is faulty, neither adequately disclosing nor concealing what is behind it. The audience never quite sees the play, although it may be stabbed nonetheless.

Other poems contain elements of the display and surreal artifice of camp: for example, doubt literally eats one away in the lines "Narcotics cannot still the Tooth / That nibbles at the soul – " (501); the ordinarily romantic moon is instead "like a Head – a Guillotine / Slid carelessly away – " (629); defeat is "populous with Bone and stain" and signifies its presence in grotesque form: "Piles of solid Moan – / And Chips of Blank – in Boyish Eyes" (639). Or, Dickinson imagines the potential of her own surrealistic dismemberment: in "There is a pain – so utter – ," her body is held up by its "open eye" and then dropped hyper-carefully "Bone by Bone" into the "Abyss" of that pain (599). Such images blur all clear separation between the human body and the rest of the world, just as they dissolve the psychological and physical glue that keeps the body whole, and the body and soul united in a stable form. All aspects of self and of perception become plastic, malleable, potentially alien to normative—that is, bourgeois, heterosexual—living.

Because such excess recognizes no boundaries in its reimagining of the self or the world, it is easier to follow Sontag's lead and focus on its sheer energy or the aesthetics of its extravagance, to marvel at the fantastic quality of individual metaphors, than to speculate on what stimulates such excess. But as contemporary feminist, lesbian, and gay critics argue, such excessive play with language and form does not stem simply from release of energy or imagination. These critics see the outrageousness of camp humor, or art, as taking its force from the double consciousness of being always in and outside of mainstream culture: lesbians may "pass" as straight in public while always being aware of their difference, and of the exclusionary consequences that would follow any public manifestation of their private choices. Camp humor provides a mode for depicting one's self in so exaggeratedly normative a way that it becomes deviant, and hence calls all cultural systems of judgment or norms into question.

In particular, recent feminist and lesbian writing on camp provides insight into Dickinson's dislocations and dissections of the body. Elaine Marks argues that in trying "to displace the phallus," (lesbian) writers must propose "a new imagery"; "to undomesticate women would mean to change the relationship between nature and culture and seriously to alter the configuration of culture as we knew it. This can only be realized through the creation of images powerful enough to impress themselves on the reader's mind and to resist the pressures of misinterpretation" (370, 372).[20] Picking up and elaborating on Marks' language, Teresa de Lauretis focuses specifically on reimagining the body: "to undomesticate the female body one must dare reinscribe it in excess—as excess—in provocative counterimages sufficiently outrageous, passionate, verbally violent and formally complex to both destroy the male discourse on love and redesign the universe" (165). Dickinson's language of excess and her fantastic, sometimes even violent, metaphors of physical substance constitute attempts to reconfigure the relationship of nature to culture, or "redesign the universe."

According to de Lauretis, such yoking of linguistic experiment and attempts to redefine the self with metaphors that reimagine the body is inevitable when one attempts to depart from gender and sexual codes.

> The struggle with language to rewrite the body beyond its precoded conventional representations is not and cannot be a reappropriation of the female body as it is, domesticated, maternal, oedipally or pre-oedipally en-gendered, but is a struggle to transcend both gender and "sex" and recreate the body other-wise: to see it perhaps as monstrous, or grotesque, or mortal, or violent, and certainly also sexual, but with a material and sensual specificity that will resist phallic idealization and render it accessible to women in another sociosexual economy. (167)

Sexuality in Dickinson's poetry tends to take a polymorphous form; rather than reinscribe sexuality in excess, Dickinson represses most mention of the body as explicitly sexual.[21] Nonetheless, the polymorphous corporeality if not sexuality of disjointed body parts in the landscape of Dickinson's poems moves beyond any pre-coded imagination of selfhood: think again of her marble self with its "chiselled" tunes, her "dropped" brain, the moon as a guillotined head, hunger like a "Claw," and her body held up by its "open eye" and dropped "Bone by Bone." Together, they suggest a pervasive, decultured, and denaturalized corporeality as radical for Dickinson's time as are the more explicit sexual mappings of camp in the twentieth century.[22]

As de Lauretis suggests, and as I stated previously, Dickinson's project of reimagining her primarily non-heterosexual woman's self involves transcending or breaking codes of gender as much as those of sexuality. Given her life choices and her era, in fact, gender would have had a far more pervasive effect on Dickinson's life than sex, and hence be a more important rule-system to explode.[23] While most nineteenth-century attempts to explode gender restrictions took the form of advocating the peculiar strengths of woman's nature and woman's sphere, Dickinson's takes the more radical form of exploding altogether the convention of a woman's sphere. In her poems of grotesquerie, her most anarchistic imaginings of a self in the world, Dickinson seems to prefer a non-, or grotesquely, gendered self. In this sense, these poems of excessive or grotesque humor are unlike other of her poems (where she makes repeated use of conventionally gendered metaphor and activity), unlike most work by her contemporaries, and also unlike camp production, which tends to exaggerate the characteristics of stereotyped roles to the point of ludicrousness. Through the grotesque humor of corporeal displacement or dismemberment, Dickinson presents the self in a way to resist all precoded conventions.

One of Dickinson's most grotesque exaggerations of corporeal presence occurs in "The name – of it – is 'Autumn'," which displaces an apparently non-gendered physical self across a whole landscape rather than isolating a single feature or distorting the relation of one body part to another. Here Dickinson presents autumn colors as a blood bath, and the landscape as a body cut open for surgery or dissection.[24]

> The name – of it – is "Autumn" –
> The hue – of it – is Blood –
> An Artery – upon the Hill –
> A Vein – along the Road –
>
> Great Globules – in the Alleys –
> And Oh, the Shower of Stain –
> When Winds – upset the Basin –
> And spill the Scarlet Rain –
>
> It sprinkles Bonnets – far below –
> It gathers ruddy Pools –
> Then – eddies like a Rose – away –
> Upon Vermillion Wheels –   (656)

This poem begins with the chill of a gothic mystery: dashes interrupt the movement from phrase to phrase so that one learns piecemeal that "it" is named autumn and has the color of blood. Once the verse reaches the ghoulish climax of "Blood," however, it moves with gusto into its theme for the next three lines, pointing out an "Artery," "A Vein," and "Great

Globules." At this point, the tone shifts again. The flippant casualness of "Oh, the Shower of Stain"—anticipated in the exaggerated, alliterative "Great Globules" and leading to the untidy accident of an overturned "Basin"—turns the grotesque gothic narrative into a sentimental domestic one. The poem's suspenseful beginning, with its heightening quotation marks and repetition, undercuts slightly the potential seriousness of the poem's theme, but the casual domesticity in stanza two is in utter disparity with any serious presentation of autumn as a time of death—the image Dickinson makes shockingly corporeal at the beginning of the poem. In this poem, Dickinson describes what is normally thought of as a melancholy or beautiful season—and perhaps more profoundly, her own melancholy or fear of death—as both grotesque and sentimental comedy. She camps through the triple play of framing narratives or expectations.

Again here, gender bears an indirect relation to the focus of the poem. The mutilated body of the landscape is non-gendered ("it") and even implicitly inhuman because of its abstract name ("Autumn"). As body, however, it is distinctly human (seasons don't have veins, arteries, blood that can clot) and its effects are gendered doubly in the poem: by the "feminine" language of coyness and sentimentality that perceives the body, and by the fact that it sprinkles "Bonnets" rather than top hats, or houses. This bloody body "Stain[s]" women before it "eddies . . . away." Together the voice of the speaker and the object stained suggest that women are somehow linked with this bloody landscape—perhaps in a grotesque play on the age-old association of women and nature revitalized by Wordsworth and other Romantic poets familiar to Dickinson; here the woman is landscape as victim, or as all too vulnerable flesh, rather than as seductively feminine inspiration ("virgin" landscape or muse). One might even imagine a link with menstruation here. The phenomenon this poem describes is peculiarly harmless (the blood becomes rose-like, eddying away upon "Vermillion Wheels"), and it recurs "when[ever]" wind spills the "Basin": blood repeatedly "Rain[s]," "gathers"—or, according to a variant, "stands" in pools—and then recedes—all in the simple present of repeated events. Here is the female body writ large, seasonally raining blood on its own head—albeit in sentimentalized form. Yet the very harmlessness and humor of the ending, with its fairytale transformations, are so at odds with the opening visual images of a body cut open across the horizon and blood oozing from the sky that a sense of mystery or uneasiness remains. Whether a reference to women's periodic bloody release, autumn's annual blood-like anticipation of winter deaths, or to some more intensely personal, repeated bloody display of the self or some other across an entire vista of earth and sky, the poem suggests a speaker who is aware of a power she will not give away. The source of the bloody bath, the identity of the body, is as secret as menstruation and yet apparently also as common to one who knows how to see.

As in "These are the Nights that Beetles love" (1128), Dickinson provides a more pointed comic or non-serious frame for this poem than for several of her others. There are no rules here as clearcut as "A Bomb upon the Ceiling / Is an improving thing" and there is no explicit mention of "merriment," but the diction throughout is that of glee and, after the first six lines, the imagery is domestic ("upset the Basin," "spill," "sprinkles Bonnets," "ruddy Pools," and so on). The trappings of the poem suggest that its opening and primary metaphor is harmless, or less grotesque than it would otherwise seem, at the same time that they cannot utterly cover its visual and psychological shock.

"Split the Lark – and you'll find the Music" (861), discussed by Juhasz in Chapter 2, contains another prolonged description of the body split open—first as a player piano and then in gory detail:

> Split the Lark – and you'll find the Music –
> Bulb after Bulb, in Silver rolled –
> Scantily dealt to the Summer Morning
> Saved for your Ear when Lutes be old.
>
> Loose the Flood – you shall find it patent –
> Gush after Gush, reserved for you –
> Scarlet Experiment! Sceptic Thomas!
> Now, do you doubt that your Bird was true?   (861)

This body is all blood—a "Flood" of "Gush after Gush" of "Scarlet"—the capital letters punctuating the gushing that occurs with each heartbeat or breath. And the speaker's dramatic demonstration is pure camp. With metaphors of frugality and business ("Scantily dealt," "Saved," "patent," "reserved"), the speaker makes the splashiest display possible of her loyalty—here, literally, the stuff she is made of—and then crows to her "Thomas" that the bloody experiment was worthwhile since it proves her right as well as "true." One has the sense that in pulsingly "Scarlet" death as well as in life, this speaker is altogether too powerful in her willfulness and her desires for her cautious lover.

Perhaps to a greater degree than other of her poems, Dickinson's poems of grotesquerie, her poems that border on camp, have a flavor of arrogance that has not been associated with women writers—especially those as gender conscious as Dickinson.[25] These poems in no way hesitate before their audience. Their extravagance presents a kind of challenge, a dare to the reader to let go of as many inhibitions on free thought as the speaker has, to share her range for reconceiving the smallest and largest aspects of social and sexual organization. These poems have a more public ring than Dickinson's poems of direct, singular address; poems written to "you" or suggesting intimacy in their diction or approach tend not to contain the same extremities of self-representation or to collapse boundaries between self and world, or body and world as these poems do. This suggests that, like camp, Dickinson's poems of excess are intended as performances. While one may tease or clown for an individual as well as for a larger audience (as Juhasz and Smith show), or while one may design a specific guise for a singular audience (Dickinson's "Uncle" to her nephew Ned), one needs a largely anonymous or non-individuated audience for poems of extreme dissonance or disruption.

Dickinson's humor of excess both does not go as far as camp and goes farther. Because it does not stem from a single aspect of experience, and because it does not partake of a community's deliberate and theatrical rejection of the cultural mores that outlaw its chosen mode(s) of living, her humor is not as pointedly critical as camp, not as barbed or direct in its wit. The diffuseness of Dickinson's humor, however, may also give it a deeper range than one normally associates with camp.

When Karl Keller reads Dickinson, he imagines himself "in bed with" her, then concludes "I notice she has not noticed me here . . . at all" (*Feminist Critics* 79). I would argue that in her poems of excess, Dickinson maintains such a distance between reader and speaker that it would be difficult to imagine oneself in close proximity to her—let alone in bed. The reader is part of the audience at a show, the (probably small) crowd that has come to watch a superb but little-known artist perform. The poems do not seem to assume that the reader will be simply shocked—that is, they are not coy in their presentation. By the same token, and although they titillate with their ambiguities and sexual play, they do not seem to want simply to entice or draw the audience into close identity. These are not poems of striptease but of continuous re-masking: there is, finally, no body exposed, no truth revealed, no self given over to the crowd. Borrowing Eco's notion of the "ideal" intended reader as this figure might be constructed from the structure of these poems, the reader is one who can share in extremes of emotional response but is more inclined to view each of the speaker's poses ironically.[26] The poems desire a reader who is as willing to be suspended between high seriousness, high hilarity, and ironic distance as the poet herself.

This paradox in apparently demanded response (extreme emotionality yet intellectual distancing) resembles, and hinges upon, the paradox in the speaker's self-presentation. She is so directly present, so outrageously physically at hand that she becomes almost (or at times literally) disembodied, without gender, difficult to perceive. By telling too much, dealing in excess, she tells nothing at all about the self one might expect her to reveal, or to see. The reader who can only conceive the speaker as sincere, as transparently truth-telling, will never hear humor in these poems—will never be "adequate" (again in Eco's terms) to this mode of Dickinson's several shows.

There is a further twist to the relation of audience to speaker in these poems determined by the fact that the reader in effect performs each poem for her or himself. To refer to a poem's "speaker" at all metaphorically disguises most of our primary contact with Dickinson's poems. While we may hear them read occasionally by other performers, and may read them aloud ourselves, we most often face a poem on the page, where the only voices speaking, the only inflections, come from the italics of our own brains. While this, too, holds true for all literature in part, it is a matter of crucial importance in Dickinson's poetry, where the voice of the poem is almost always distinctly spoken but where there are few if any clues as to the identity or personality of a dramatic speaker. The poems are not "dramatic monologues" in a traditional sense any more than they are simply confessional narratives. All Dickinson's poems demand a reader who is willing to step into the poem in order to understand it, a reader who will not wait for the poem or poet to present its (her) self. Because of their tension between elements of sincerity or seriousness and elements of humor, Dickinson's poems of excess demand a reader willing to "speak" and hear the poem multiply for him or herself.

One may see this quality of display in each of the poems discussed above. In "I like a look of Agony" and "I measure every Grief I meet," the speakers reveal aspects of themselves so unusual as to call into question their reason for such revelation. The reader does not peep into a private corner of the speaker's soul, or eavesdrop on private conversation, but witnesses an emotional exhibitionist in mid-performance. "This is what I do, what I like," she proclaims, asserting with absolute certainty the truths on which she bases her assumptions, and leaving no implied room for audience response or questioning. In "These are the Nights that Beetles love," "We dream – it is good we are dreaming," and "The name of it – is 'Autumn,'" the speaker describes conditions besides (or not exclusively) her own, but the idiosyncrasy of the descriptions again puts the reader at a distance: this is an Autumn, an insect-filled summer night, or a version of the old cliché that "life is a dream" that we have not experienced before and perhaps do not want to share. The sensibility that sees strewn leaves as a dissected corpse, a "Bomb upon the Ceiling" as desirable, or life as a double game of "kill us" and "shriek" flaunts itself, inviting as much shock or admiration at its boldness as participation or sympathy. Similarly, in the descriptions of "A still – Volcano – Life" and "She dealt her pretty words like Blades," the speaker reveals a kind of glee in knowing what the "North cannot detect" and in dismissing human pain as "old Custom." The speaker is not interested in politeness but in "glittering" or in volcanic honesty that simultaneously reveals and devastates. Again, there is no place for community of understanding, or exchange of expression, here. A knife wielder's or volcano's audience is "wanton[ly]" tormented or destroyed. One hears a yet clearer expression of this tone in "Dare you see a Soul *at the White Heat?*" (365), with its invitation to the reader to "crouch within the door," and its proclamation of difference. "Red – is the Fire's common tint – ," and the color of (common—not "blue") blood. Dickinson, however, here proclaims her (superior, aristocratic) ability to suffer fire or intensity so hot within her soul that it is "Without a color, but the light / Of unanointed Blaze." In "I cannot dance upon my Toes," Dickinson writes of her art as being "full as Opera" (326). In these poems, she borrows the trappings and quality of staged performance, including that of opera, the most artifice-ridden of arts.

The stage of public performance protects an actor from personal or immediate audience response. "It was only a role," the actor may say; "I am not the person I played." Similarly, these poems of Dickinson's suggest that she creates a protection similar to that of the stage for herself. In her circumstance of privileged person writing poetry she will not publish, Dickinson creates a context of privacy, idiosyncrasy that forestalls most kinds of criticism (even Higginson will not criticize strictly to her what his "pupil" indicates she does not intend to publish). At the same time, the gesture or manner of these poems of excess create their own stage by distancing the reader through a flamboyant display of their subject or object. In these poems Dickinson is doubly or triply distanced from those she addresses: through lack of publication (or pretense that the poems are written for her benefit only); through the off-putting display of the poems themselves; and through the claim she makes explicitly to Higginson (and may repeat to others) that the poems do not "represent" herself anyway (L 268).

Writing long before the philosophically proclaimed death of either God or the author, Dickinson often sees her rebellion in existential terms—against a patriarchal order more powerful than that of human institutions and men. As an essentially postmodern writer in a Romantic era, rather than assuming her beliefs about multiplicity, doubt, structures that do not hold, and conventions that do not explain, Dickinson must argue them; and her vocabulary for these arguments inevitably draws from the lexicons of the culturally embedded institutions she would reject. Similarly, Dickinson—unlike producers of contemporary camp—is as apt to attempt to create a new space for herself in the natural as in the social, cultural world. While she will overlay nature with conventions of perception which suggest that it is no more a refuge than any other socially defined sphere, Dickinson also returns repeatedly to nature in her poems as a place to learn about herself as well as a place for the largest canvas of self-display. In this sense, her concern ceases to be (the postmodern) with roles or conventions of representation and becomes more a (Romantic) concern with what might be called essence—the most profound sense of who and what kind of thing she is.

Humor in the form of excess, by definition, stands outside any rule or law—including, perhaps, critical definitions of comedy or humor. It makes its audience wonder whether the author hasn't gone too far, perhaps shouldn't be joking about a particular topic, or perhaps isn't joking. As a text, such humor may make a reader laugh uncontrollably in the context of one reading and then be utterly baffled as to why it seemed funny in the context of another. In part, such humor demands excess from the reader: only if he or she is also willing to let go of prescribed boundaries separating the serious, the zany, the grotesque, the sentimental will the reader gain entrance to this marginal edge of wildness that constitutes humor in a number of Dickinson's poems. These poems are themselves products of neither excess (one does not suspect Poe-esque doses of laudanum or opium behind the text) nor hysteria: as works, they stem from a poet's control. Nonetheless, they are works where Dickinson may risk more in the areas of consistency, tone, or logical coherence than in most of her oeuvre, in order to express more fully than otherwise her rejection of the conventions of embodiment, gender, propriety, selfhood that would restrict her life. Emily Dickinson's poems of humorous excess constitute an important part of her lifelong production because such excess reveals with stark clarity tendencies of thought and response present in milder or more controlled form in much of this extremely versatile poet's verse.

Chapter 5
Comic Power

THROUGH TEASE, CARTOONING, and grotesquerie, Dickinson critiques and disrupts cultural conventions and regulations. She takes the normalizing frames of our world and unhinges them, forcing them askew to make space for a joke, for a different take. Calling her assumptions and our own into question, her comic poems challenge all manners of orthodoxy. Peculiar, sly, witty, dry, shocking, slapstick, ridiculous, even gory, these are serious poems that are comic in their interrogation of authority, in the way they break or subvert the rules. They are comic in another sense as well: they offer the possibility of lasting transformation rather than, in the way of traditional comedy, advocating a return to conventional strictures. Dickinson's humor reshapes the components of the world that she knows, so that the poem becomes a site for a transforming vision; her comic speakers, like the storyteller of "Before I got my eye put out" (327), invite us to participate in radically alternative scenarios.

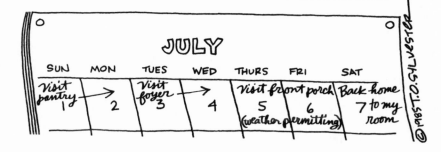

In appreciating Dickinson's transforming vision, we should acknowledge that one aspect of the transformation occurs in our vision of the poet herself. The Dickinson who is capable of striptease, cartoons, and excessive grotesquerie is not the well-known tragic heroine. Her performances take a comic turn. Imagine her up there on the stage, with the wit and hutzpah of Mae West, the bravado of Carol Burnett, and the drollery of Lucille Ball: the "Placard[s] boast" her (326). This Dickinson, doing her American Express TV commercial routine, quips: "I never leave home, but I'm never without it!" Smoothing her skirt, she continues: "Why the white dress, you want to know? People have always made it into such a big deal: because I wanted to be a nun, because I had a terrible skin disease, because like Miss Havisham I was pining away for my groom to come. Fact is, it was simply that Austin and Sue owned the first grass court in America. Tennis, anyone?" The first lady of the witty wisecrack can shimmy, she can ridicule, she can terrify. Like a good stand-up comic she can transform our world-view—both while we're applauding her jokes and afterward. We may have closed the book, but we are not the same.

What kind of poetic transformation does this comedienne bring about? When her "Bird [comes] down the Walk" (328), for example, this feathered friend does not sweetly sing. Nor does he pine, like the nightingale, over past sorrow. He spots an Angleworm, bellies up to the sushi bar, and eats the fellow, raw. Then, having savored his snack, this little carnivore, like a proper New England gentleman, steps aside to let a beetle pass, all the while glancing around guiltily, as though this courtesy were about to get him in big trouble. No typical nineteenth-century songbird herself, Dickinson wickedly disturbs a clichéd vision of nature through her ornithological caricature.

This is disruption—that is, traditional comedy—but not yet transformation. That occurs quite literally in the poem when the speaker moves from the frame of observation onto the stage of performance and "Cautious, / . . . offer[s] him a Crumb":

> And he unrolled his feathers
> And rowed him softer home –
>
> Than Oars divide the Ocean,
> Too silver for a seam –
> Or Butterflies, off Banks of Noon,
> Leap, plashless as they swim.

Within this poem we experience several kinds of transformation. First, we see this Romantic symbol of poetic flight as capable of everyday meanness. Later, however, we witness that ordinary creature altered yet again, as he becomes the focal point for a vision of a new home. Time and space shift dimensions; disparate elements—water, sky, and earth—unify seamlessly; and the result is a playground of possibility. The bird, like a butterfly, swims, sails, leaps, flies, soars into a bright meridian. If Dickinson's comedy stems from profound discomfort with society as it has been constructed, and her comic strategy destabilizes that construction, often by defamiliarizing it, then her transformations sketch the outlines of a world that more readily suits her aspirations. Like this bird in glorious flight, or like the bird, "shut . . . up in Prose" who "Abolish[es] his Captivity"(613) through laughing, Dickinson frees herself through the flight of her imagination, through "Conversions of the Mind" (593).

As with all good comedy, the transformation does not stop with the poet or her poems, those "Tomes of solid Witchcraft" (593). While for each reader the "Conversion" may be different, even as the experience of reading is different for each individual, it is the lingering of that new personal vision that hooks so many of us. Dickinson likens these conversions to "Sanctifying in the Soul" as well as a "Divine Insanity." One reader explains it as a change in the way she conceives of the very limits of experience. Dickinson has stretched it, twisted it, turned it inside out. What *are* the Banks of Noon anyway? What can it mean to row him softer home? You can see it, you can feel it, you get a shiver of delight every time you read it—but those lines of poetry do not make literal sense. As a consequence, they evoke something outside of ordinary experience—something that feels right, at once safe and beautiful: something toward which this reader can only aspire, for which she can only hope. Dickinson calls it a Jubilee suddenly confirmed. It's in the poem; it's in the reader's mind. It isn't factual, but it is definitely *there*.

For another reader, the transformation is primarily linguistic, opening new perspectives on the world through an understanding of what more radically than Keats' "negative capability" encourages bafflement, wonder, a belief in sorcery, and acceptance of the unknown. At the same time, this linguistic transformation makes the new or unknown analogous to the familiar through wonderful slant rhymes ("adorned" with "confirmed" and "Sane" with "turn" in "I think I was enchanted," or "face" with "Paradise" in "Her Sweet turn to leave the Homestead" [649]). Dickinson gives us ways of arranging and creating words that make us see "Mighty Metres . . . / The Homeliest – adorned" (593), even when the change is in part terrifying in its strange disjunctiveness.

Another direction in which the reader's transformations can occur is in thinking about the poet herself. If Dickinson was indeed this funny, this wild, this shrewd, this bold, slapstick, even campy on some occasions, then what does this mean for interpreting the rest of her life? For example, what about the enigmatical quotations from Shakespeare that she sent next door to her closest friend, Sue Dickinson? Might not they, too, be informed by her humor? Consider, for example, "Egypt – thou / knew'st" (L 430), the opening for Antony's impassioned speech to Cleopatra and often interpreted by critics as an avowal of love, with Sue as Emily's Cleopatra. Yet when put in the context of Dickinson's brazen humor and with full awareness that the two houses shared many things—including daily Shakespeare calendars—a reader cannot help but imagine that these unsigned, unaddressed written quotations ferried from one Dickinson house to another might well have been part of an elaborate game concocted by the two literary women. Maybe this was some nineteenth-century form of *Jeopardy*—"I gave the answer," Emily quips, "now you, Sue, supply the question."

Admitting such a possibility may seem a little matter, but so much has been made of the sadness in those houses and of the supposed misery of Dickinson herself, that it is really no small thing at all. Turning our eyes to Dickinson's comedy humanizes her, makes her that much more believable, palpable, and wise. It expands her range, her significance, and her power. For Emily Dickinson the comedienne is, after all, the same poet as Emily Dickinson the tragediennne. Clearly, she writes poems expressing profound sorrow and psychological trauma or pain. But this reading of the poet does not account for her equally pronounced and profound affirmation of life, and it is in the affirmative force of many of her poems that the crux of Dickinson's comic vision is revealed. Dickinson breaks up the old order to create a new order, a new home, which is the poem itself. Just as she literally cuts up others' books to illustrate her own poems, or paraphrases lines that then suffer a sea-change in the context of her own words, so she re-structures the world outside her door, not destroying it so much as rearranging it. In doing so, she revels in the literary act that enables her re-creations, her linguistic pyrotechnics attesting to her sense of performance, of going public on the page, and this very emphasis upon the performative status of her writing invites our readerly participation in making and inhabiting the poem. This is comic power, a transformative magic which, as Dickinson tells us, "hath an Element / Like Deity – to keep – " (593).

©1987 T.O.SILVESTER

FEATURING:

- A CONDO IS
  A SMALL DOMAIN

- THERE IS NO FRIGATE
  LIKE A VCR

- BECAUSE I COULD NOT STOP FOR DEBT
  IT KINDLY STOPPED FOR ME

Notes

Chapter 1. Comedy and Audience in Emily Dickinson's Poetry

1. Gary Lee Stonum's recent study of Dickinson's rhetoric, *The Dickinson Sublime*, shows clearly how Dickinson's own theory of poetry was a theory of affect, of the response of the reader to a poetry constructed so as to engender such responses.

2. Walker does say, however, that since the 1970s, women's and men's humor have become more similar—presumably because of women's increasing prominence in every walk of public life (*A Very Serious Thing* 14).

3. Walker apparently ignores here Eco's claim that comedy is ultimately the more conservative form, as it only pretends to provide freedom in its explosion of the rule while in fact reinstating some new version of the old regime. Both Walker and Regina Barreca tend to collapse the distinctions between feminist and women's humorous writing in their works, although both admit that the difference exists. Walker makes her distinction largely in response to Gloria Kauffman and Mary Kay Blakely, who draw a sharp distinction, observing in women's humor an upbeat attitude that is accepting of women's position and power, as opposed to the sharper perspective of feminist humor, which condemns a situation that doesn't appear to be changing. See *Pulling Our Strings: Feminist Humor and Satire*, quoted in Walker 149–150 and passim.

4. See Nancy Walker's "Emily Dickinson and the Self: Humor as Identity" for a more complete review of the wit, whimsy, satire, and irony in Dickinson's verse.

5. We have chosen the variant of poem 288 published in *The Complete Poems of Emily Dickinson*, edited by Thomas H. Johnson (Boston: Little, Brown, and Co., 1960), 133. All subsequent references to Dickinson's poems are to *The Poems of Emily Dickinson*, edited by Thomas H. Johnson, 3 vols. (Cambridge, Mass.: The Belknap Press of Harvard University Press, 1955) or to *The Manuscript Books of Emily Dickinson*, edited by R. W. Franklin, 2 vols. (Cambridge: The Belknap Press of Harvard University Press, 1981). References to this volume use either "F" and fascicle number or "Set" and set number.

Chapter 2. The Big Tease

1. Gary Lee Stonum, in *The Dickinson Sublime*, addresses issues of Dickinson's relation to "mastery" in terms of the romantic sublime. His work is clearly pertinent to this discussion, especially as it studies Dickinson's disinclination both to be "mastered" by her subject matter and to "master" her reader. "Reading and writing, like most other acts in Dickinson's world, are always vulnerable to some form of a master-slave relation. More specifically, authorial control is usually for Dickinson a mark of the author as Master" (15). Stonum's analysis of how Dickinson creates a poetic program to circumvent mastery is especially valuable as it defines her focus on a poetics of affect, "stimulating responses without dictating them" (48). However, while he examines at length Dickinson's techniques to evade mastering her reader, he does not explore her fear of her reader's mastering her, nor does he look at the relation of gender to any of these matters.

2. Dorothy Huff Oberhaus refers to the relation between riddle and Dickinson's poetry in "Dickinson as Comic Poet" in *Approaches to Teaching Dickinson's Poetry* (119).

3. Jane Eberwein, following Rebecca Patterson, points out a more specific reference for Dickinson's use of "Exeter":

> Dickinson went back to the British legend of the lord of Burleigh to provide the context for her poems on sudden coronation. The heroine of that tale was a humble village maiden married to a seemingly ordinary man who escorted her after their simple wedding to his presumably modest home some distance from her village. Approaching Burleigh House after long travel, she asked who owned it—only to hear from her husband, now revealed as the tenth earl, "It is all yours, and you are the countess of Exeter." (101)

Eberwein also notes that Dickinson's tendency to see herself as queen or earl almost always involves a recent elevation to dignity: "The notion of coronation delighted Dickinson" (100).

4. "Adopting the pose of a child, Dickinson can challenge authority by assuming ignorance," writes Mossberg in *Emily Dickinson: When a Writer Is a Daughter* (121).

5. Discussing Dickinson's teasing of her reader, Domhnall Mitchell describes Dickinson "offering clues which do not lead where we expect them to. Despite the insistent preoccupation with speaking [in poem 812] the poem is a 'show' and not a way to 'know' " (209).

6. Gary Lee Stonum discusses at length Dickinson's sense of an "elite" reader, to whom he feels all of her poems are addressed. He quotes another "Ear" poem that distinguishes between elite and ordinary readers:

> Reportless Subjects, to the Quick
> Continual addressed –
> But foreign as the Dialect
> Of Danes, unto the rest.

Reportless Measures, to the Ear
Susceptive – stimulus –
But like an Oriental Tale
To others, fabulous –   (1048)

While Stonum is aware that there are two categories of readers, he does not discuss what lies behind their differing reading skills. "Programmatically unwilling to dictate how her work was to be taken, she was thus content to create the poetic stimuli in the hopes that the appropriate respondents might appear" (106).

7. Domhnall Mitchell writes about Dickinson's use of "play," which I would associate with her tease: "it becomes a means for overcoming the panic and terror that pervades the darkest poems on death, turning them instead into strategies for ordering that which cannot be ordered" (218).

8. Gary Lee Stonum finds another such "rare and wondrous vision of mutuality" in the conclusion of poem 1651, "A Word made Flesh is seldom." The vision is specifically related to a fit between reader and language: "the word naturally fits our specific strength," he writes, continuing: "the uncanny match perhaps suggests that the word's power depends on how strongly we can respond to it" (97).

9. Cristanne Miller, in *Emily Dickinson: A Poet's Grammar*, notes this grammatical ambiguity, commenting: "The uninflected verb 'consume' may further temper the poem's suggestion of ultimate human vulnerability. So far I have read the line 'Experience either and consume – ' as though the second verb is the threatened effect of the first: if you experience you will (be) consume(d). The two verbs may, however, represent parallel directions: 'Experience either and consume' (either poetry or love). Consume, in this reading, specifies what happens when you 'experience': to taste of either poetry or love is to devour either" (129–130). And Gary Stonum, commenting on the same issue, observes: "Construed as a transitive verb, 'consume' presupposes taking love or poetry into the self from the outside. The word cannot fully hold off its participial complement, however, a reversed sense in which experiencing the sublimity of love or poetry entails being consumed. 'Prove' has a similar reversible transitivity, love and poetry putting us to the proof fully as much as we them" (156–157).

Chapter 3. The Poet as Cartoonist

1. *Emily Dickinson: Friend and Neighbor* (128–129).

2. Herblock writes for the *Washington Post* and Ben Sargent for the *Austin American-Statesman*.

3. See "Loomings" (Chapter 1), *Moby-Dick*.

4. Indicating awareness that the personal is political and that many private issues are not so separate from public ones after all, many cartoons complicate their subject matter. *Doonesbury* uses the private and public lives of numerous characters to underscore political critiques that concern the society and the individual, as do the otherworldly portrayals in *Outland*, which happily (thus repeatedly) make the

point that culture teems with basic genetic differences, not just differences of opinion. Sadly, looking at the comic strips of any Sunday American newspaper (in this case that of the *Washington Post*) to learn about life in these United States, a reader would conclude that ours is an almost exclusively white society and was preceded by societies that were exclusively white, even in the most primitive stages (*B.C.*, e.g.); the exceptions to this are few. Some examples are: Berke Breathed's *Outland* and Lynn Johnston's *For Better or Worse* often foreground at least one character of color, and Garry Trudeau's *Doonesbury* sometimes does as well.

5. Though Shira Wolosky persuasively argues that Dickinson was in fact deeply engaged with the world around her, most notably the Civil War, she does not critique her humorous political commentary. See *Emily Dickinson: A Voice of War*. Betsy Erkkila, on the other hand, has recently claimed that Dickinson "set herself against the abolitionist, reformist, and democratizing energies of the times" (7) and that the poet's "elitism is evident in her almost complete silence on the major social issues of her time" (9). In making her argument, Erkkila relies heavily on the reports of Thomas Higginson and Mabel Loomis Todd and ignores important evidence such as Karen Dandurand's discovery that some of Dickinson's poems were contributed to a "wartime fund-raising paper called the *Drum Beat*" (18); more importantly, Erkkila ignores many of Dickinson's direct commentaries on politics, the most significant of which are her lifelong complaints about her disenfranchised status as a woman. When the poet was twenty-one, she opined, "Why cant *I* be a Delegate to the great Whig Convention? – dont I know all about Daniel Webster, and the Tariff, and the Law?" (L 94), then three decades later sardonically observed that "Little Boys are commemorating the advent of their Country" (L 650, discussed below; references to Dickinson's letters are to the Johnson and Ward edition and will use "L" and give the number assigned by Johnson). Erkkila may be projecting the elitist views of Higginson and Loomis Todd back onto Dickinson.

Dickinson's niece Martha Dickinson Bianchi writes about her aunt's political humor in the introduction to her first edition of Emily Dickinson's poems (*The Single Hound*, xiii–xiv).

6. An 1851 cartoon from *Punch* featured in the June issue of *Harper's* and alluded to in one of Emily's letters to Austin is reprinted by Jay Leyda (1 : 201). An 1869 cartoon with which Dickinson may have been familiar, especially since Frederick Olmsted landscaped both the Evergreens and Amherst College, is one criticizing Olmsted's plans for the pastoral order of Central Park, reproduced by Lawrence W. Levine in *Highbrow/Lowbrow: The Emergence of Cultural Hierarchy in America* (205).

7. Illustrated children's periodicals like *Parley's Magazine* were part of the family's reading material as well (Leyda 1 : 45). As a reader of *Harper's*, Dickinson surely saw its December 1859 feature "Spriggin's Voyage of Life," a cartooning pictorial narrative directly alluding to Thomas Cole's influential series of paintings *The Voyage of Life* (discussed below). Judith Farr recently reproduced this cartoon (72–73). Dickinson may have also been familiar with "the pictorial narrative of

the medieval Bayeux tapestry, the eighteenth-century print series of such artists as William Hogarth and Thomas Rowlandson, the illustrated European broadsheet," also credited as sources for the comic strip (Inge 76). For a brief history of the comic strip's evolution, see M. Thomas Inge, "What's So Funny about the Comics?" in *American Humor*, ed. Arthur Power Dudden (76–84). Inge's essay is a valuable resource on the history of the comic strip's evolution, as is Dudden's compilation of works on American humor by Peter M. Briggs, Alan Gribben, Lawrence E. Mintz, Joseph Boskin and Joseph Dorinson, Nancy Walker, and Stephen J. Whitfield. See also, David Kunzle, *The History of the Comic Strip: The Nineteenth Century*, and Judith O'Sullivan, *The Great American Comic Strip*.

8. In *Rowing in Eden*, I propose that we pay attention to the care both Emily and Sue Dickinson take to distinguish between the terms "publish" and "print," then entertain the possibility that she considered sending poems out in letters and making the little books we now call fascicles kinds of "publication." She sent at least one-third of her poems out in letters, and, while she bundled them together and left orders to destroy all letters from her correspondents after she died, she left no such instructions regarding the manuscript books.

9. As we indicated in the opening chapter, poems reproduced by R. W. Franklin in *The Manuscript Books of Emily Dickinson* are indicated by "F" or "Set" and the fascicle or set number (given by Franklin) only. Throughout this chapter, I follow Dickinson's lineation, which Johnson changed, whenever possible. My reasons for being as faithful to the manuscript as typographic reproduction can be are extensively discussed in *Rowing in Eden*.

10. The one-woman show is William Luce's *The Belle of Amherst*; Charles Kuralt narrated the one-minute spot for CBS (it has not been shown, though he has discussed the poet on *CBS Sunday Morning*); the L.P. is *Emily Dickinson—A Self-Portrait*; the murder mystery is Jane Langton's *Emily Dickinson Is Dead*; and the cookbook is by Guides at the Dickinson Homestead, *Profile of the Poet as Cook*. The paragraph below refers to Paul Simon, "The Dangling Conversation," *Parsley, Sage, Rosemary & Thyme*. For an expanded analysis of the uses of the figure Emily Dickinson, see the concluding paragraphs of "To Fill a Gap," the first chapter of *Rowing in Eden*.

11. Van Dyke goes on to point out that in 1981 David Porter claimed that the "seclusion chose the art, rather than the artist the seclusion." (*Dickinson* 119). In this instance he is arguing with feminist poet Adrienne Rich who had asserted that Dickinson "chose her seclusion, knowing she was exceptional and knowing what she needed" ("Vesuvius at Home" 160).

12. In his first essay on Dickinson, R. P. Blackmur concluded that she "wrote indefatigably as some women cook or knit" and that "her gift for words and the cultural predicament of her times drove her to poetry instead of antimacassars" ("Notes on Prejudice and Fact" 223). Even in his later essay on her in which he argues for her complexity in technique and compares her punctuation to the notes of music, Blackmur concluded that "we cannot say of this woman in white that she ever mastered life—even in its loosest metaphor" ("Emily Dickinson's Notation"

85). Similarly, David Porter concludes that "the crucial affair for [Emily Dickinson], rather, is living after things happen," and he also characterizes her as a "compulsive writer but without a conscious objective that a notebook or a versebook would have indicated" (*Dickinson* 9, 83).

13. March 23, 1891, letter, quoted by Millicent Todd Bingham (*Ancestors' Brocades* 118). Manuscripts at the Houghton Library, Harvard University, will be indicated by the initial "H" and the library catalog letter and/or number.

14. A frequent essayist in periodicals like the *Atlantic Monthly* and the *Woman's Journal*, Higginson wrote extensively on American culture, abolition, women writers, and women's rights. The first quotation here is from his 1859 *Atlantic Monthly* essay "Ought Women to Learn the Alphabet," the second from "Study and Work," both of which are reprinted in *Women and the Alphabet*. Lawrence W. Levine both quotes from Higginson's 1866 *Atlantic Monthly* essay "A Plea for Culture" and points out that Higginson defines culture in a "resolutely classical and European-oriented manner" and often appends the term with the adjective "high."

15. In a section on "minor" women writers, Higginson describes Emily Dickinson in a paragraph and reproduces a facsimile of his copy of "Safe in their Alabaster Chambers" (Higginson and Boynton 130–131).

16. Of women writers and poets like those presented by Griswold, Higginson says, "Young girls appear one after another: each writes a single clever story or single sweet poem, and then disappears forever. . . . Nobody doubts that women have cleverness enough" (*Women and the Alphabet* 231).

17. Critical treatment of *Uncle Tom's Cabin*, nineteenth-century America's best seller, provides a perfect literary example of how popular literature has traditionally been devalued in the academy as second-rate. See Jane Tompkins, "Sentimental Power" (122–146).

18. For discussion of the cultivations common for women of Dickinson's class (like tending a conservatory with a wide range of flowers, ferns, and exotic plants and making herbariums), see Jean McClure Mudge, *Emily Dickinson and the Image of Home* (esp. 145–172), and St. Armand's presentation of Martha Dickinson Bianchi's unfinished essay, "Emily Dickinson's Garden" in *Emily Dickinson International Society Bulletin*.

19. As Huyssen points out, Tania Modleski analyzes the relationship of the production/consumption paradigm in "Femininity as Mas(s)querade: A Feminist Approach to Mass Culture." For a complementary analysis of the threat to the pretensions of "high" art raised by late twentieth-century popular culture, see Martha Nell Smith, "Sexual Mobilities in Bruce Springsteen: Performance as Commentary."

20. In an 1853 letter to Austin, Lavinia mentions reading Fanny Fern's work to their father: "Father was *thoughtful* enough to spend last evening with us *socially* & as he seemed rather dull, I endeavored to entertain him by reading spicey passages from Fern leaves, where upon he brightened up sufficiently to correct me as I went

along, advising me to put in all the little words as they would'nt hurt me &c. You can imagine the rest as you have heard such like before" (Bingham *Home* 312).

21. Manuscripts at Amherst College will be indicated by the initial "A" and the library catalog number.

22. To compare handwriting, readers should consult Franklin's facsimile reproduction of *The Master Letters of Emily Dickinson* (esp. 21–29). In *Rowing in Eden*, I examine this cartoon specifically in relation to the "Master" letters.

23. Various impacts of the nineteenth-century notions and theories of separate spheres for male and female have been studied by a wide variety of critics. One of the most influential has been Nancy Cott's *The Bonds of Womanhood: "Woman's Sphere" in New England, 1780–1835*. For commentary attending specifically to American women poets, see Cheryl Walker, *The Nightingale's Burden: Women Poets and American Culture before 1900* (esp. 21–58).

24. For example, Mary Ann C. McGuire overlooks the ironies suggested by this poem in "A Metaphorical Pattern in Emily Dickinson." Jack L. Capps also appears to read the poem as an uncritical response to "the image of Little Nell's mourning grandfather" (97–98).

25. References to Dickinson's prose fragments reproduced in Johnson and Ward's edition of her letters will use "PF" and give the number assigned by Johnson.

26. Interpreting Dickinson's strategies to impel the reader beyond conventional endings, I am consciously echoing Rachel Blau DuPlessis' examinations of women writers' strategies, though I argue that these tactics appear in women's works long before 1900 and, for that matter, long before Dickinson; see *Writing beyond the Ending: Narrative Strategies of Twentieth-Century Women Writers*.

27. I discuss the editing of this poem at length in both *Rowing in Eden* and "Gender Issues in Textual Editing of Emily Dickinson"; also see note 32.

28. In *The Passion of Emily Dickinson*, Judith Farr, as did St. Armand, reproduces several paintings of which Dickinson would have been aware, among them Cole's series *The Voyage of Life* (plates following p. 208).

29. Rourke first characterized Dickinson in this way (209–210). Walker opens her essay by reiterating Rourke's assertion.

30. Dickens' use of inanimate objects to suggest such things as the "quaint gaiety of a forbidden life and an aggressiveness that has got out of control" has long been discussed (Van Ghent 129).

31. Kristeva is, of course, elaborating Freud's proposition (Hogarth edition 8:179–180).

32. When Loomis Todd produced what St. Armand describes as "user-friendly" editions of Dickinson's works, she also emphasized and through her editing produced "user-friendly" stories of the poet Higginson called "that virgin recluse." Late nineteenth-century audiences were prepared to receive and adore a female poet harboring "secret sorrow," and suggestions that Dickinson was yet another of these have served both as text and subtext since the earliest printings of her

work. For example, in the 1896 edition of *Poems by Emily Dickinson*, Loomis Todd underscored her change of "A solemn thing – it was – " (F 14; P 271) to a two-stanza poem celebrating matrimony and titled "Wedded" (she excised the last two stanzas) by titling "He fumbles at your Soul" (F 22; P 315) "The Master," and situating it to center the section of poems she titled "Love." Though the Higginson-Todd-Bingham school of reception and the Dickinson-Bianchi-Hampson school have each accused the other of perpetuating the "Myth" of the lovelorn poetess Dickinson, they are both responsible. Most frequently, Bianchi bears the brunt of negative commentary regarding this, but Loomis Todd and Bingham participated in construction of this image as much as she. The most salient factor for readers embarking on a second century of Dickinson study is that the reclusive poetess in white was the version of Emily Dickinson most easily commodified, and that all forementioned parties profited from their reproductions of her works.

33. William H. Galperin's study of this poem's reception offers some vital insights into developments in Dickinson study in general and feminist critiques of Dickinson in particular.

34. See, e.g., Jerome McGann's "The Text, the Poem, and the Problem of Historical Method," and Sharon Cameron's discussion in *Lyric Time* (esp. 121–135), both discussed by Galperin.

35. See Hans Robert Jauss' well-known essay "Literary History as a Challenge to Literary Theory." Horizons can be either "fixed and unalterable" (as in Christian epistemology) or "movable and changing" (as in the modern experience of the world). Obviously, I am drawing upon the idea of the open horizon, "that every current horizon gives way to new horizons as one moves along or travels," and I do not concur with critical views that would close interpretation of this poem off in Christian epistemology. "From a hermeneutic point of view, the divide between the closed horizon of expectations of innerworldly knowledge and the open horizon of onmoving experience corresponds to the divide between understanding as the recognition and interpretation of a professed or revealed truth on the one hand, and understanding as the search for or investigation of a possible meaning on the other" (Jauss, *Question and Answer* 200).

36. Cynthia Griffin Wolff has recently argued that in the mid-1860s or early 1870s Dickinson gained the faith in God and immortality that she had for so long doubted (504–507). Also, critic Ellen Louise Hart furthers an argument broached by Rebecca Patterson and Paula Bennett that Dickinson hoped to join Sue in the "'Costumeless Consciousness' (H 358; P 1454) of immortality, the mind without the body, limitless, free of artifice and the restrictions of gender" (264).

37. Criticisms offering such interpretation are: John Cody, (180–181); Clark Griffith (177–183, 215, 284–288); Mudge (104–108).

38. The characterization of Dickinson comes from repeated analysis of an early letter to Sue (L 93, 1852). But in their later correspondence, Dickinson welcomes the sun, which she now identifies with Sue (L 755), and her adolescent expressions of fears of masculinity virtually disappear.

39. For analysis of Blake, see Jerome McGann (47). Though it remains under-studied, talked about but not critiqued, Sue's involvement with Emily's literary production has long been recognized; their famous exchange over "Safe in their Alabaster Chambers" proves Sue's influence (see P 216 & L 238); when Sue sees the poem published in the *Republican*, she writes, "*Has girl read Republican?* It takes as long to start our Fleet as the Burnside" (HB 94 and Johnson, *Interpretive Biography* 117). "*Our* Fleet" suggests mutual endeavor. That Sue was deeply engaged with Dickinson's writing is clear from letters written in the 1860s by editor and dear friend Samuel Bowles. In 1862, he implores Sue to "tell Emily to give me one of her little gems!" Two years later one of his letters may even suggest that the women are writing together: "Speaking of writing, do you & Emily give us some gems for the '*Springfield Market*,' & then come to the Fair" (Leyda 2:68, 93). Readers might consult my discussion in "Dickinson's Poetry Workshop," Chapter 5 of *Rowing in Eden*.

Chapter 4. The Humor of Excess

1. I make this comment largely in response to a group of critics, most articulately represented by David Porter in *The Modern Idiom*, who see much of Dickinson's work as accidental or containing elements of naïve linguistic confusion. I argue, in contrast, that these poems are functionally irrational, hence ultimately coherent, not confused. Porter does not discuss most of the poems I treat at length in this chapter, but these belong to the type of which he is most critical. For example, he refers to the phrase "a Dome of Abyss is Bowing / Into Solitude" in "How the old Mountains drip with Sunset" (291) as "apparent humbug" (31).

2. In *They Used to Call Me Snow White*, Regina Barreca claims it is typical of women to make fun of those in high and seemingly invulnerable positions rather than of scapegoat figures (13). See David Reynolds' *Beneath the American Renaissance*, especially the chapter "The Carnivalization of Language," for information on nineteenth-century grotesque humor.

3. Those interested in the relation of Dickinson's grotesquerie to so-called "black humor" should see David Reynolds' and Neil Schmitz' work on American humor. An illuminating comparison of Dickinson's to Samuel Beckett's humor might also be made. While I greatly admire Reynolds' work, as the preceding paragraph implies, I strongly disagree with his assumption that because Dickinson may borrow heavily from male (and often misogynistic) popular writers she therefore cannot be rebelling "against fixed patriarchal systems" (427). To me, this sounds suspiciously like saying that because Dickinson borrows heavily from the Bible in her style and in allusion, she cannot be criticizing God or Christian culture as practiced in her day. Like biblical syntax, savage humor is a stylistic tool that may be used to any purpose.

4. As will become clear from the following discussion, I am not using the term "excess" in Georges Bataille's sense of "unconditional expenditure" or obsession (*Visions of Excess* 118). There are, nonetheless, occasional points of overlap between

the excessive meaning and language play of Dickinson's work and the obsessive focus on what exceeds limits in Bataille. For example, Bataille's proposition that "laughter only assumes its fullest impact on being at the moment when . . . a representation of death is cynically recognized," with its correspondent claim that "laughter attains not only the peripheral regions of existence . . . [but] through a necessary reversal, it is sent back from the child to its father and from the periphery to the center," helps explain Dickinson's use of the grotesque in her humor. She appears to recognize the capacity of humor, or laughter, both to express the margin of her own radical critique and momentarily to restructure or reverse the order of things such that it becomes temporarily central (176–177).

5. In previous work on Dickinson's language, I have described similar linguistic and metaphorical gaps in her poems in relation to multiply recoverable syntactic deletions (see *A Poet's Grammar* and "Dickinson's Language: Interpreting Truth Told Slant"). In part, this term would also cover the kind of excess I refer to here. Where linguistic and narrative excess are combined so that one must recreate the poem's sentences in order to imagine the scene or perception of the speaker—generally a process requiring more than one recreation—the structure may indeed be multiply recoverable. Single metaphors of excess, however, are multiply and incongruously suggestive without syntactic or logical deletion: the compression is ready-made in the metaphor. Multiply recoverable deletion is a poet's strategy for creating a certain kind of poetics, and may appear in extremely different types of poems. Humor of excess and grotesquerie are matters of content and degree; they partake more clearly of political or social than of formal strategy.

6. I am indebted to the students of a graduate seminar I taught on Dickinson at the University of Michigan, Ann Arbor, for my reading of this poem.

7. *A Subtreasury of American Humor* (1945), quoted in *A Very Serious Thing*, xi–xii.

8. Here Mellencamp is quoting from Sigmund Freud's *Jokes and Their Relation to the Unconscious* (Norton & Co. edition), 228, 231, 228.

9. In the nineteenth century, women writing humorous fiction or poetry did not write of dislocated body parts strewn across the landscape or macabre death and pain fantasies; outside of the gothic tradition, they did not write in such a mode at all.

10. On Dickinson and landscapes, see Suzanne Juhasz, *The Undiscovered Continent*, and Christopher Benfey, *Emily Dickinson and the Problem of Others*. Juhasz explores the extent to which all landscapes in Dickinson's poems are internal, and Benfey presents Dickinson as a poet who reads the human body as she reads landscapes. Neither discusses Dickinson's tendency to see isolated parts of her (or a woman's) body IN the landscape.

11. The 1986 film *Matador* has especially striking parallels with this poem—where sex and torture or death are inseparable for most of the characters, and the movie ends in a hilariously parodic or camp scene of two murderers making love in an attempt to achieve doubly simultaneous orgasms and murders/deaths.

12. In *A Poet's Grammar*, I write about the possibility that the victim in "He

fumbles at your Soul" is preparing herself for the "imperial blow" while she waits for it to come (115–118). In "The Soul has Bandaged moments," the speaker escapes in the middle stanzas of the poem; because the soul "has" such moments repeatedly, there is a suggestion that the sequence of events is always the same: capture, escape, recapture.

13. "Walt Whitman Camping" (7). The phrases quoted above are taken from Keller's definitions of camp as a "critical/analytical tool" and as it appears in literature. Later on this page he describes Dickinson as camping when she "plays little girl before God and vamp to the Creation: as she put it, she was 'the only Kangaroo among the Beauty.' "

14. Esther Newton (1972) and Laud Humphreys (1972) define camp as constantly changing and hence in some ways as indefinable: if it were to become static and therefore appropriable by mainstream (straight) culture, it would cease to be camp.

15. Sontag sees the androgyne as a central image of camp, and links camp sensibility to (male) homosexuality, although again vaguely and without any conscious reading of the politics of androgyny, or sexual play. Because she defines camp as "innocent" (apolitical), she finds no serious reference to gender or sexual roles in its "play," and sees merely exaggeration rather than distortion in its images. Critics who align camp with the gay and lesbian communities insist on the political aspects of its role playing and wit.

16. Humphreys also compares camp to soul as the primary and defining characteristic of the homosexual and black communities respectively, and as incorporating what he calls "skills of the oppressed" strategically developed over time by those communities (63–73).

17. Typically regarded (and most often written about) in the context of male homosexuality, camp is not, and historically has not been, an exclusively male form. Although the drag-queen constitutes camp's most widely recognized and publicly acceptable player, and although there is no widely known, performing equivalent to this flamboyant figure in the lesbian community (there are relatively few professional drag-butches or male impersonators, and they are not popularly associated with outrageousness or humor), camp forms have been traced in early twentieth-century lesbian production and are present in current work. See Newton's *Mother Camp* for an overview and analysis of camp (street) display and professional performance. Early twentieth-century lesbian works displaying elements of camp include Djuna Barnes' *The Ladies Almanack* and *Ryder*, and Renée Vivien's stories. More widely known, the famous women's blues singers of the 1920s and 30s (Ida Cox and Bessie Smith in particular) camp in their outrageous allusions to and manipulations of women's roles and (lesbian and straight) sexuality (see, for example, Hazel Carby's "It Jus Be's Dat Way Sometime: The Sexual Politics of Women's Blues").

Keller's essay may contribute to the stereotype that a woman camps only within the context of a masculine interpretation and gaze in that he sees Dickinson's campiness as her teasing play to a male audience. "Imagining her audience to be male," Keller argues, "gave Emily Dickinson opportunity to play the deviant. Perhaps she could have played that among women, too, but she would not have had to be as brisk, as nasty, as coy, as teasing, as sure" ("Sleeping with Emily Dickinson" 67, 70). Dickinson uses her art to dissemble; in an age where all serious literary endeavor was male, she is "trying to hide the fact that she is a woman," using her "poetry for stuffing": "This is not dishonest, just marketing-necessity. In a man this art would be a hoot. In a woman it is camp" (71).

Despite Keller's masculine frame, talking about Dickinson's poems as camp does not necessarily place her in the context of male homosexual culture or audience; it places her instead in the context of a diverse twentieth-century community's choices to manifest its radical difference from mainstream culture through flaunting, aggressive, and humorous displays of alternative roles or codes for behavior.

18. In particular, Dickinson's work is not "wholly aesthetic"; she does not use in primary ways the metaphor "of life as theatre" nor does she encourage a cult of personality or individual mannerisms instead preferring a more internalized and abstract form of excess (Sontag 287, 290). Newton's definition is anachronistic for Dickinson, as there was no lesbian (or homosexual) community as such through which she might have defined herself (Dickinson could not possibly have thought of herself as a lesbian in the contemporary sense); in fact, for women, there appears to have been no stigma of deviance attached to loving other women over and above men—although such love was not culturally defined as sexual. See Carroll Smith-Rosenberg, "The Female World of Love and Ritual" in *Disorderly Conduct*, Lillian Faderman's *Surpassing the Love of Men*, and Esther Newton's "The Mythic Mannish Lesbian: Radclyffe Hall and the New Woman."

19. For a discussion of the possible psychological background of Dickinson's hunger poems, see Barbara Mossberg, especially the chapter "Hunger in the House," and Norbert Hirschhorn.

20. While Marks argues that no one has managed to create such images before Monique Wittig, Sue-Ellen Case finds powerful reconfigurations of culture in all butch-femme role playing. Working from current notions of the "female subject" as culturally bound, Case argues that the redefined, "coupled" (not split) female subject-role(s) of the butch-femme "lend[s] agency and self-determination to the historically passive subject, providing her with at least two options for gender identification and, with the aid of camp, an irony that allows her perception to be constructed from outside ideology, with a gender role that [nonetheless] makes her appear as if she is inside of it." According to Case, butch-femme roles utterly disrupt the phallic order: superficially, the butch "proudly displays the possession of the penis, while the femme takes on the compensatory masquerade of womanliness" yet both roles are foregrounded by the fact that these are two women playing to each other; hence "there is no referent in sight; rather, the fictions of penis and castration become ironized and 'camped up' . . . these women play on the phallic economy rather than to it" (292–293). One might argue that Dickinson, alternately, takes on both butch and femme roles in her poetry, although in less theatrical ways than the modern lesbian community would recog-

nize. Certainly in these poems she primarily "plays on the phallic economy rather than to it."

21. For example, the largest number of Dickinson's sexually focused poems use bees and flowers or other natural phenomena to present heterosexual or autoerotic patterns of relationship. Sexuality adheres in the landscape rather than in the human body. One would anticipate this in her poetry given her daily guise of asexuality—almost acorporeality—perhaps expressed in her references to herself as wearing white.

22. It is, as Reynolds states, Dickinson's use of such violent grotesquerie in (apparently or in fact) serious poems that distinguishes her writing from that of contemporary subversive humorists. This very thin line between serious social critique and humor also makes the kinds of poems I am discussing here closer to camp productions than to nineteenth-century grotesque humor.

23. See John D'Emilio and Estelle Freedman on the changing discourses of sexuality in the United States. Before the 1920s and 30s, women were not likely to think of sexual fulfillment or of sexual experience generally as crucial to their well-being or happiness. See Carroll Smith-Rosenberg on the complex relations of passionlessness as ideology, the sphere of womanhood, women's rights advocacy, and the desire to be non-gendered as they develop and change during the mid- and late nineteenth century.

24. For my sense of the humor and the tone of this poem, I am indebted to Joanne Diehl's and Barbara Packer's extended readings and discussion of the poem at the 1986 conference "Emily Dickinson: A Celebration for Readers," reprinted in Juhasz and Miller (87–113).

25. It may be, however, that Dickinson fits the profile for a comic woman writer better than for women writers generally, or especially for women poets. According to Alice Sheppard, most "prominent women humorists" of the nineteenth century came from established families in New England, were well-educated, and "showed streaks of rebellion and mischief in their characters" ("The Social Context of Women's Humor," 160–61). The same does not seem to have been true of women poets (see Cheryl Walker's *The Nightingale's Burden*). This arrogance might also in part come naturally to the daughter of Amherst's leading lawyer and a national congressman (for a term). Dickinson seems to have enjoyed fully the privileges of her race, wealth, and class, without being altogether conscious of them.

26. See Eco's *The Role of the Reader*. I do not mean that this is a model reader, far less that this is the only way one might read Dickinson's poems. This is, however, the way I am attempting to read them as well as (circularly) the way that I see the poems as structuring my readings.

Works Cited

Barnes, Djuna. *The Ladies Almanack*. Printed for the Author and sold by Edward W. Titus. Facsimile ed. New York: Harper and Row, 1972.

———. *Ryder*. New York: St. Martin's Press, 1956.

Barreca, Regina. *They Used to Call Me Snow White . . . but I Drifted: Women's Strategic Use of Humor*. New York: Viking Penguin, 1991.

———, ed. *Last Laughs: Perspectives on Women and Comedy*. New York: Gordon and Breach, 1988.

Barthes, Roland. "From Work to Text." In *Image—Music—Text*, translated by Stephen Heath. New York: Hill & Wang, 1977.

———. *SZ*. Translated by Richard Miller. London: Jonathan Cape, 1974.

Bataille, Georges. *Visions of Excess. Selected Writings 1927–1939*. Edited by Allan Stoekl. Minneapolis: University of Minnesota Press, 1985.

Benfey, Christopher. *Emily Dickinson and the Problem of Others*. New York: St. Martin's Press, 1988.

Bennett, Paula. *My Life a Loaded Gun: Female Creativity and Feminist Poetics*. Boston: Beacon Press, 1986.

Bianchi, Martha Dickinson. "Emily Dickinson's Garden." Edited by Barton St. Armand. *Emily Dickinson International Society Bulletin* 2, No. 2 (1990), 1–2, 4.

———. *The Life and Letters of Emily Dickinson*. Boston and New York: Houghton Mifflin, 1924.

———, ed. *The Single Hound*. See under Dickinson, Emily.

Bingham, Millicent Todd. *Ancestors' Brocades: The Literary Debut of Emily Dickinson*. New York: Harper and Brothers Publishers, 1945.

———. *Emily Dickinson's Home: Letters of Edward Dickinson and His Family*. New York: Harper and Brothers Publishers, 1955.

Blackmur, R. P. "Emily Dickinson: Notes on Prejudice and Fact." In *The Recognition of Emily Dickinson: Selected Criticism Since 1890*, edited by Caesar R. Blake and Carlton F. Wells, 201–223. Ann Arbor: University of Michigan Press, 1964.

———. "Emily Dickinson's Notation." In *Emily Dickinson: A Collection of Critical Essays*, edited by Richard B. Sewell, 78–87. Englewood Cliffs, N.J.: Prentice-Hall, Inc., 1963.

Cameron, Sharon. *Lyric Time: Dickinson and the Limits of Genre*. Baltimore: The Johns Hopkins University Press, 1979.

Capps, Jack L. *Emily Dickinson's Reading, 1836–1886*. Cambridge, Mass.: Harvard University Press, 1966.

Carby, Hazel. "It Jus Be's Dat Way Sometime: The Sexual Politics of Women's Blues." *Radical America* 20, no. 4 (1986), 9–24.

Case, Sue-Ellen. "Toward a Butch-Femme Aesthetic." In *Making a Spectacle: Feminist Essays on Contemporary Women's Theatre*, edited by Lynda Hart. Ann Arbor: University of Michigan Press, 1989.

Charney, Maurice. "Comic Creativity in Plays, Films, and Jokes." In *Handbook of Humor Research*, vol. 2, edited by Paul E. McGhee and Jeffrey H. Goldstein, 33–40. New York: Springer-Verlag, 1983.

Cody, John. *After Great Pain: The Inner Life of Emily Dickinson*. Cambridge, Mass.: The Belknap Press of Harvard University Press, 1971.

Cott, Nancy. *The Bonds of Womanhood: "Woman's Sphere" in New England, 1780–1835*. New Haven and London: Yale University Press, 1977.

Culler, Jonathan. *Structuralist Poetics: Structuralism, Linguistics, and the Study of Literature*. Ithaca: Cornell University Press, 1975.

Dandurand, Karen. "New Dickinson Civil War Publications." *American Literature* 56 (March 1984), 17–27.

Davidson, Cathy N. *Revolution and the Word: The Rise of the Novel in America*. New York and Oxford: Oxford University Press, 1986.

D'Emilio, John, and Estelle Freedman. *Intimate Matters: A History of Sexuality in America*. New York: Harper & Row, 1988.

de Lauretis, Teresa. "Sexual Indifference and Lesbian Representation." *Theatre Journal* 40 (May 1988), 155–177.

Dickinson, Emily. Dickinson Papers, Houghton Library, Harvard University; and Frost Library, Amherst College.

———. *The Letters of Emily Dickinson*. Edited by Thomas H. Johnson and Theodora Ward. 3 vols. Cambridge, Mass.: The Belknap Press of Harvard University Press, 1958.

———. *The Manuscript Books of Emily Dickinson*. 2 vols. Edited by R. W. Franklin. Cambridge, Mass.: The Belknap Press of Harvard University Press, 1981.

———. *The Master Letters of Emily Dickinson*. Edited by R. W. Franklin. Amherst, Mass.: Amherst College Press, 1986.

———. *The Poems of Emily Dickinson*. Edited by Thomas H. Johnson. Cambridge, Mass.: The Belknap Press of Harvard University Press, 1955.

———. *The Single Hound: Poems of a Lifetime*. Edited by Martha Dickinson Bianchi. Boston: S. J. Parkhill and Co., 1914.

Diehl, Joanne Feit. "Terrains of Difference: Reading Shelley and Dickinson on Autumn" and "Workshop Discussion." In *Emily Dickinson: A Celebration for Readers*, edited by Suzanne Juhasz and Cristanne Miller, 87–90, 95–113. London and New York: Gordon and Breach, 1989.

Dobson, Joanne. *Dickinson and the Strategies of Reticence: The Woman Writer in Nineteenth Century America*. Bloomington: Indiana University Press, 1989.

Dudden, Arthur Power, ed. *American Humor*. New York and Oxford: Oxford University Press, 1987.

DuPlessis, Rachel Blau. *Writing beyond the Ending: Narrative Strategies of Twentieth-Century Women Writers*. Bloomington: Indiana University Press, 1985.

Eberwein, Jane Donahue. *Dickinson: Strategies of Limitation*. Amherst, Mass.: University of Massachusetts Press, 1985.

Eco, Umberto. "The Frames of Comic 'Freedom.'" In *Carnival!*, edited by Thomas A Sebeok. Berlin: Mouton Pubs, 1984.

———. *The Role of the Reader: Explorations in the Semiotics of Texts*. Bloomington: Indiana University Press, 1979.

Emily Dickinson—A Self-Portrait. New York: Caedmon Records, Inc., 1968.

Erkkila, Betsy. "Emily Dickinson and Class." *American Literary History* 4 (Spring 1992), 1–27.

Faderman, Lillian. *Surpassing the Love of Men*. New York: William Morrow & Co., 1981.

Farr, Judith. *The Passion of Emily Dickinson*. Cambridge, Mass., and London: Harvard University Press, 1992.

Franklin, R. W., ed. *The Manuscript Books of Emily Dickinson*. See under Dickinson, Emily.

———. *The Master Letters of Emily Dickinson*. See under Dickinson, Emily.

Freud, Sigmund. *Jokes and Their Relation to the Unconscious*. Translated by James Strachey. New York: Norton & Company, 1960.

———. *Jokes and Their Relation to the Unconscious. The Standard Edition of the Works of Sigmund Freud*, vol. 8. Edited by James Strachey. London: Hogarth Press & the Institute of Psychoanalysis, 1960.

Frost, Robert. "Education by Poetry." In *Robert Frost: Poetry and Prose*, edited by Edward Connery Lathem and Lawrence Thompson, 329–340. New York: Holt, Rinehart and Winston, Inc., 1972.

Fulton, Alice. *Powers of Congress*. Boston: David R. Godine, 1990.

Fussell, Paul. *Poetic Meter and Poetic Form*. New York: Random House, 1965.

Galperin, William H. "Emily Dickinson's Marriage Hearse." *Denver Quarterly* 18 (1984), 62–73.

Gay, Peter. *The Bourgeois Experience: Victoria to Freud. Education of the Senses*, vol. 1. New York: Oxford University Press, 1984.

Gilbert, Sandra M. "The Wayward Nun beneath the Hill: Emily Dickinson and the Mysteries of Womanhood." In *Feminist Critics Read Emily Dickinson*, edited by Suzanne Juhasz, 22–44. Bloomington: Indiana University Press, 1983.

———, and Susan Gubar. *The Madwoman in the Attic: The Woman Writer and the Nineteenth-Century Literary Imagination*. New Haven: Yale University Press, 1979.

Goodman, Joel. "How to Get More Smileage Out of Your Life: Making Sense of

Humor, Then Serving It." In *The Handbook of Humor Research*, vol. 2, edited by Paul E. McGhee and Jeffrey H. Goldstein. New York: Springer-Verlag, 1983.

Griffith, Clark. *The Long Shadow: Emily Dickinson's Tragic Poetry*. Princeton: Princeton University Press, 1964.

Griswold, Rufus, ed. *The Female Poets of America*. Philadelphia: Carey and Hart, 1849.

Guides at the Dickinson Homestead. *Profile of the Poet as Cook*. Amherst, Mass.: Hamilton I. Newell, Inc., 1976.

Harris, Julie. *Emily Dickinson—A Self Portrait*. Directed by Howard Sackler. New York: Caedmon Records, Inc., 1968.

Hart, Ellen Louise. "The Encoding of Homoerotic Desire: Emily Dickinson's Letters and Poems to Susan Dickinson, 1850–1886." *Tulsa Studies in Women's Literature* 9 (Fall 1990), 251–272.

Higginson, Thomas Wentworth. *Women and the Alphabet: A Series of Essays*. Boston and New York: Houghton Mifflin Co., 1900.

———, and Henry Walcott Boynton. *A Reader's History of American Literature*. Boston, New York, and Chicago: Houghton, Mifflin and Company, 1903.

Hirschhorn, Norbert. "A Bandaged Secret: Emily Dickinson and Incest." *The Journal of Psychohistory* 18, no. 3 (Winter 1991).

Humphreys, Laud. *Out of the Closets: The Sociology of Homosexual Liberation*. Englewood Cliffs, N.J.: Prentice-Hall, 1972.

Huyssen, Andreas. "Mass Culture as Woman: Modernism's Other." In *After the Great Divide: Modernism, Mass Culture, Postmodernism*, 44–62. Bloomington and Indianapolis: Indiana University Press, 1986.

Inge, M. Thomas. "What's So Funny about the Comics?" In *American Humor*, edited by Arthur Power Dudden, 76–84. New York and Oxford: Oxford University Press, 1987.

Jauss, Hans Robert. *Question and Answer: Forms of Dialogic Understanding*, edited and translated by Michael Hays. Minneapolis: University of Minnesota Press, 1989.

———. "Literary History as a Challenge to Literary Theory." In *Toward a Theory of Reception*, translated by Timothy Bahti, 3–45. Minneapolis: University of Minnesota Press, 1982.

Jenkins, MacGregor. *Emily Dickinson: Friend and Neighbor*. Boston: Little, Brown, and Company, 1930.

Johnson, Thomas H. *Emily Dickinson: An Interpretive Biography*. Cambridge: Belknap Press of Harvard University Press, 1955.

———, and Theodora Ward, eds. *The Letters of Emily Dickinson*. See under Dickinson, Emily.

Juhasz, Suzanne, ed. *Feminist Critics Read Emily Dickinson*. Bloomington: Indiana University Press, 1983.

———. *The Undiscovered Continent: Emily Dickinson and the Space of the Mind*. Bloomington: Indiana University Press, 1983.

—— and Cristanne Miller. *Emily Dickinson: A Celebration for Readers*. London and New York: Gordon and Breach, 1989.

Kauffman, Gloria, and Mary Kay Blakely. *Pulling Our Strings: Feminist Humor and Satire*. Bloomington: Indiana University Press, 1980.

Keller, Karl. "Notes on Sleeping with Emily Dickinson." In *Feminist Critics Read Emily Dickinson*, edited by Suzanne Juhasz. Bloomington: Indiana University Press, 1983.

——. *The Only Kangaroo among the Beauty: Emily Dickinson and America*. Baltimore: Johns Hopkins University Press, 1979.

——. "Walt Whitman Camping." *Odyssey* 4 (November 1979), 6–11.

Kristeva, Julia. "Laughter as Practice." In *Revolution in Poetic Language*, translated by Margaret Waller. New York: Columbia University Press, 1984.

Kunzle, David. *The History of the Comic Strip: The Nineteenth Century*. Berkeley: University of California Press, 1990.

Langton, Jane. *Emily Dickinson Is Dead*. New York: St. Martin's Press, 1984.

Levine, Lawrence W. *Highbrow/Lowbrow: The Emergence of Cultural Hierarchy in America*. Cambridge, Mass., and London: Harvard University Press, 1988.

Leyda, Jay. *The Years and Hours of Emily Dickinson*. 2 vols. New Haven and London: Yale University Press, 1960.

Luce, William. *The Belle of Amherst*. Boston: Houghton Mifflin, 1976.

Lystra, Karen. *Searching the Heart: Women, Men, and Romantic Love in Nineteenth-Century America*. New York: Oxford University Press, 1989.

McConnell-Ginet, Sally. "Women's Words: Negotiating Meaning." Unpublished paper delivered at Pomona College, 26 January 1989.

McGann, Jerome. *A Critique of Modern Textual Criticism*. Chicago and London: University of Chicago Press, 1983.

——. "The Text, the Poem, and the Problem of Historical Method." *New Literary History* 12 (1981), 269–288.

McGhee, Paul E., and Jeffrey H. Goldstein, eds. *Handbook of Humor Research*. New York: Springer-Verlag, 1983.

McGuire, Mary Ann C. "A Metaphorical Pattern in Emily Dickinson." *American Transcendental Quarterly* 29 (Winter 1976), 83–85.

Marks, Elaine. "Lesbian Intertextuality." In *Homosexualities and French Literature: Cultural Contexts / Critical Texts*, edited by George Stambolian and Elaine Marks. Ithaca and London: Cornell University Press, 1979.

Mellencamp, Patricia. "Situation Comedy, Feminism, and Freud: Discourses of Gracie and Lucy." In *Studies in Entertainment*, edited by Tania Modelski, Bloomington: Indiana University Press.

Merrill, Lisa. "Feminist Humor: Rebellious and Self-Affirming." In *Last Laughs*, edited by Regina Barreca. New York: Gordon and Breach, 1988.

Miller, Cristanne. *Emily Dickinson: A Poet's Grammar*. Cambridge, Mass.: Harvard University Press, 1987.

——. "Dickinson's Language: Interpreting Truth Told Slant." In *Approaches to*

Teaching Dickinson's Poetry, edited by Robin Riley Fast and Christine Mack Gordon. New York: MLA, 1989.

Mitchell, Domhnall. *Emily Dickinson and the Limits and Possibilities of Critical Judgement*. Diss. Trinity College, Dublin 1989.

Modleski, Tania. "Femininity as Mas(s)querade: A Feminist Approach to Mass Culture." In *High Theory, Low Culture*, edited by Colin McCabe. Manchester: University of Manchester Press, 1986.

———, ed. *Studies in Entertainment: Critical Approaches to Mass Culture*. Bloomington and Indianapolis: Indiana University Press, 1986.

Mossberg, Barbara. *Emily Dickinson: When a Writer Is a Daughter*. Bloomington: Indiana University Press, 1982.

Mudge, Jean McClure. *Emily Dickinson and the Image of Home*. Amherst, Mass.: University of Massachusetts Press, 1974.

Newton, Esther. *Mother Camp: Female Impersonators in America*. Englewood Cliffs, N.J.: Prentice-Hall, 1972.

———. "The Mythic Mannish Lesbian: Radclyffe Hall and the New Woman." *Signs* 9 (Summer 1984), 557–575.

Oberhaus, Dorothy Huff. "Dickinson as a Comic Poet." In *Approaches to Teaching Dickinson's Poetry*, edited by Robin Riley Fast and Christine Mack Gordon. New York: MLA, 1989.

Ostriker, Alicia. "No Rules of Procedure: The Open Poetics of H.D." In *Signets: Reading H.D.*, edited by Susan Stanford Friedman and Rachel Blau DuPlessis. Madison and London: University of Wisconsin Press, 1990.

O'Sullivan, Judith. *The Great American Comic Strip*. Boston, Toronto, London: Little, Brown and Co., 1990.

Packer, Barbara. "Dickinson and the Contract of Taste" and "Workshop Discussion." In *Emily Dickinson: A Celebration for Readers*, edited by Suzanne Juhasz and Cristanne Miller, 91–113. London and New York: Gordon and Breach, 1989.

Poirier, Richard. *The Performing Self: Compositions and Decompositions in the Languages of Contemporary Life*. New York: Oxford University Press, 1971.

Pollak, Vivian R. *Dickinson: The Anxiety of Gender*. Ithaca: Cornell University Press, 1984.

Porter, David. *Dickinson: The Modern Idiom*. Cambridge, Mass.: Harvard University Press, 1981.

———. "Shakespeare Cartoons." *New York Times*, 2 September 1990, sec. 2:3.

Reynolds, David. *Beneath the American Renaissance: The Subversive Imagination in the Age of Emerson and Melville*. Cambridge, Mass.: Harvard University Press, 1989.

Rich, Adrienne. "Vesuvius at Home: The Power of Emily Dickinson." In *On Lies, Secrets and Silence: Selected Prose, 1966–1978*, 157–183. New York and London: W. W. Norton and Co., 1979.

Ross, Andrew. "Uses of Camp." *The Yale Journal of Criticism* 2 (Fall 1988), 1–24.

Rourke, Constance. *American Humor: A Study of the National Character*. New York: Harcourt, Brace, 1931.

Russo, Mary. "Female Grotesques: Carnival and Theory." In *Feminist Studies/ Critical Studies*, edited by Teresa de Lauretis. Bloomington: University of Indiana Press, 1986, pp. 213–229.

St. Armand, Barton. "Emily Dickinson's Garden." *Emily Dickinson International Society* 2, no. 2 (November/December 1990), 1–2, 4.

————. *The Soul's Society: Emily Dickinson and Her Culture*. Cambridge and New York: Cambridge University Press, 1984.

Sayre, Henry. "Performance." In *Critical Terms for Literary Study*, edited by Frank Lentricchia and Thomas McLaughlin. Chicago and London: University of Chicago Press, 1990.

Schmitz, Neil. *Of Huck and Alice: Humorous Writing in American Literature*. Minneapolis: University of Minnesota Press, 1983.

Sewall, Richard B. *The Life of Emily Dickinson*. New Haven and London: Yale University Press, 1974.

Sheppard, Alice. "From Kate Sanborn to Feminist Psychology: The Social Context of Women's Humor, 1885–1985." *Psychology of Women Quarterly* 10 (1986), 155–170.

Simon, Paul. "The Dangling Conversation." *Parsley, Sage, Rosemary and Thyme*. New York: Columbia Records, 1966.

Smith, Martha Nell. "Gender Issues in Textual Editing of Emily Dickinson." *Women's Studies Quarterly* 19 (Fall/Winter 1991), 78–111.

————. *Rowing in Eden: Rereading Emily Dickinson*. Austin: University of Texas Press, 1992.

————. "Sexual Mobilities in Bruce Springsteen: Performance as Commentary." *South Atlantic Quarterly* 90 (Fall 1991), 833–854.

Smith-Rosenberg, Carroll. *Disorderly Conduct: Visions of Gender in Victorian America*. New York: Oxford University Press, 1985.

Sontag, Susan. *Against Interpretation and Other Essays*, 2d ed. New York: Farrar, Straus, Giroux, 1986 (1st ed. published in 1966).

Stonum, Gary Lee. *The Dickinson Sublime*. Madison: University of Wisconsin Press, 1990.

Tompkins, Jane. "Sentimental Power: *Uncle Tom's Cabin* and the Politics of Literary History." In *Sentimental Designs: The Cultural Work of American Fiction*, 122–146. New York and Oxford: Oxford University Press, 1985.

Van Dyke, Joyce. "Inventing Emily Dickinson." *Virginia Quarterly Review* 60 (Spring 1984).

Van Ghent, Dorothy. "On *Great Expectations*." In *The English Novel: Form and Function*. New York: Rinehart and Co., 1953.

Vivien, Renée. *The Woman and the Wolf and Other Stories*. Translated by Karla Jay and Yvonne M. Klein. New York: Gay Presses of New York, 1983.

Walker, Cheryl. *The Nightingale's Burden: Women Poets and American Culture before 1900*. Bloomington: Indiana University Press, 1982.

Walker, Nancy. "Emily Dickinson and the Self: Humor as Identity." *Tulsa Studies in Women's Literature* 2, no. 1 (Spring 1983), 57–68.

———. *A Very Serious Thing: Women's Humor and American Culture*. Minneapolis: University of Minnesota Press, 1988.

Weisbuch, Robert. *Emily Dickinson's Poetry*. Chicago: University of Chicago Press, 1975.

Whicher, George Frisbie. *This Was a Poet: A Critical Biography of Emily Dickinson*. New York: Charles Scribner's Sons, 1938.

Wolff, Cynthia Griffin. *Emily Dickinson*. New York: Alfred A. Knopf, 1986.

Wolosky, Shira. *Emily Dickinson: A Voice of War*. New Haven and London: Yale University Press, 1984.

Wylder, Edith. *The Last Face: Emily Dickinson's Manuscripts*. Albuquerque: University of New Mexico Press, 1971.

Zadravec, Katharine. "Emily Dickinson: A Capital Visitor." In *Emily Dickinson: Letter to the World*, edited by Katharine Zadravec, 26–33. Washington, D.C.: The Folger Shakespeare Library, 1986. A monograph published for the Dickinson Centennial at the Folger library.

Index

Index of Poems by First Lines

Parenthetical references indicate their representation in Thomas H. Johnson's *Poems of Emily Dickinson* and R. W. Franklin's *The Manuscript Books of Emily Dickinson*. References to the Johnson edition use the initial "P" and give the number assigned by Johnson; references to the Franklin use the initial "F" or word "Set" and cite fascicle or set number only.

Index of Letters by Recipient and First Line(s) or Important Words

Parenthetical references indicate their representation in Thomas H. Johnson's *The Letters of Emily Dickinson*. References use the initial "L" and cite the number assigned by Johnson.

General Index